SEARCHING
FOR
SEEKERS

SEARCHING
FOR
SEEKERS

Ministry with a New Generation of the Unchurched

Mary J. Scifres

ABINGDON PRESS
Nashville

SEARCHING FOR SEEKERS
MINISTRY WITH A NEW GENERATION OF THE UNCHURCHED

Scifres, Mary J.
    Searching for seekers. Ministry with a new generation of the unchurched / Mary J. Scifres.
        p.   cm.
    ISBN 0-687-00552-3
    1. Worship programs. Non-church affiliated people. I. Title.
BV15.S34 1998
253—dc21   98-44291
                                                              CIP

Unless otherwise noted, all scripture quotations are from The New Revised Standard Version Bible, copyright © 1989 by the Division of Christian Education of the National Council of the Churches of Christ in the USA. Used by permission.

Hymntext of the song "I Quietly Turned to You" by Ragan Courtney and Buryl Red © Copyright 1972 Broadman Press. Assigned to Van Ness Press Inc. All rights reserved. Used by permission.

98 99 00 01 02 03 04 05 06 07— 10 9 8 7 6 5 4 3 2 1

MANUFACTURED IN THE UNITED STATES OF AMERICA

This book is dedicated to my best friend, favorite editor, and loving partner-husband, B. J. Beu. For your timeless hours reading and improving, pushing and prodding, comforting and encouraging, I thank you.

For Michael and the other Seekers who come and go in my life, I offer this book as a gift in hopes that we can travel the journey of faith together rather than alone.

CONTENTS

INTRODUCTION

Over the course of my life, I have learned much about God, life, faith, hope, and love from friends who have either left the church or who have never been to church at all. These friends encouraged me to seek God and live according to deeply held values and principles. As a Christian, I have always believed that the Church has much to offer my friends in their faith journey. As a Christian leader, I feel called to help make this belief a reality. What follows is the result of many years of yearning to find ways to welcome my friends back into the church or into the church for the first time. I dream of a nation full of churches that welcomes Seekers as we all learn together how to better love God and neighbor.

As you read through the pages ahead, you may wonder if reaching these Seekers is far beyond the grasp of the church where you live and serve. Don't get discouraged! The guidelines and thoughts in this book represent ideal situations and solutions; they should not be viewed as all or nothing. As a pastor, I have always sought to create a Seeker-friendly atmosphere in the churches where I serve. However, these churches have never satisfied all of the criteria outlined in this book to be considered completely Seeker-friendly in either worship or fellowship. But somehow, the striving has been enough. Seekers continue to drift into these churches and many find safe, accepting homes, even in the midst of our shortcomings. Simply doing what you can with love is more successful than mechanically achieving any ideal formula for the most welcoming or dramatic Seeker ministry in town.

To make the best use of this book, consider your setting and your specific worship and ministry needs. You may find it helpful to use this book as a resource, turning to specific chapters for help when the need arises. For the most practical advice on improving your current worship services or developing new ones, turn to chapter three. Chapter six is also particularly helpful if you are developing a new ministry or worship service for Seekers. To understand the different types of Seekers in our country, you will find chapter two helpful in understanding generational differences; you will also find chapter three's descriptions of different types of Seekers useful in recognizing that different types of Seekers avoid the church for different reasons. For the preacher, chapter five may be your most useful tool. And for those who want more general ideas on understanding and reaching Seekers, chapter four offers a hodgepodge of tools for doing so. If you're really in a hurry and hate reading, skip straight to Appendix A for the "shortcut" lists of Seeker-friendly ideas.

My hopes and prayers are with each reader of this book, and with each church that searches for Seekers, striving to integrate the faith journeys of Seekers and Followers so that we may all learn and grow together. Here's to the journey!

Shalom,
Mary Scifres

CHAPTER ONE

Spiritual Seekers

Developing a Passion for Seekers

As I drove my car into the Indianapolis city limits, images of Michael flashed through my mind: years of playing pranks on our church camp counselors, summers filled with talent shows and walks in the woods, quiet talks late into the night of parents and friends and other confusing relationships, long letters filled with encouragement and scripture references as we struggled through the doubts of our adolescent years, and memory upon memory of attending every significant event of one another's lives for almost 10 years. How did that friendship fade so quietly and quickly into distant memory and the lament of unfulfilled promises? I was certain that it must have been my fault—allowing our friendship to fade as I concentrated on my seminary work in faraway Boston. Now, I was back in the Midwest, going through a difficult time, and there was no one I wanted to see more than Michael.

As I arrived at Michael's dilapidated apartment that warm spring day, I learned how much my seminary years had affected him; but the story I heard was not the one I expected. After catching up on the three years we had lost, it became clear that Michael was somehow afraid of me. After years of sharing our Christian faith together, Michael had chosen a different path. He was dabbling in a bit of New Age philosophy, but mostly Michael had simply lost interest in the religious questions that had bonded us together so many years before. Michael's new life was dedicated to the pursuit of success and acceptance in a world of business and art that scorned traditional expressions of faith.

During the years I had been outgrowing our fundamentalist adolescence, Michael had been abandoning Christianity. While I had been integrating the best teachings from the world religions during my liberal arts studies in college, Michael had been giving up his childhood church that condemned his friends and colleagues to hell. Whereas I grew to accept my doubts as a part of my ongoing faith journey, Michael chose to trust in his doubts more than in his beliefs. So, as we sat and talked that afternoon in Indianapolis, I heard my best friend of so many years tell me that he wasn't sure if I still wanted to be his friend. He thought that I would no longer want to spend time with him since so much of my life was now wrapped up in an institution he had rejected. His doubts in God became doubts in our friendship, perhaps because he equated me as more godly than he or perhaps because he thought that a believer would not want to associate with a doubter. Just as he was no longer sure he could trust the church, he seemed no longer sure whether he could trust me. I was stunned.

Here was a man who had been nurtured in his faith by a little country church that loved him abundantly. He had been raised in an accepting and loving home, with parents who regularly discussed other religious outlooks on the world. For years, he and I had attended church camp together, where we learned through the exploration of Broadway musicals that the sacred and secular were not mutually exclusive realities. How was it that I—the feminist preacher—could feel safer in the church than he did?!

That was the day my interest in Seekers ceased to be an academic exercise and became a passionate reality. That was the day I knew that part of my calling is to search for Seekers, to reach out to the Michaels of the world.

On that bright afternoon as we wandered the desolate grounds of his apartment complex, I realized that the unchurched person would never fit a single stereotype. These days, I cringe every time I read another book that labels "Seekers" as hostile to the church, anti-Christian in outlook, secular and hedonistic in their value system, and ignorant of the message of the Christian Gospel. Anger and frustration swell up within me when I read another article that claims "Seekers" are incapable of worshiping God. During that long afternoon conversation with Michael about life and morality, spiritual journeys and faith questions, I realized that non-Christians are seldom non-religious.

When I reflect on my crowd of friends from the small United Methodist college I attended, I see two groups of people: one group who either became pastors or married pastors and one group who left the church. What happened to the University of Indianapolis Class of 1987? Did the lack of required chapel threaten our entire future in the Christian faith? Did the stringent rules of dorm-life drive us from the institutional church? Or, did an accumulation of life experiences coupled with busy schedules allow, even encourage, us to drift away from any religious upbringing that had first brought us to a small, Christian, liberal arts college?

Many of the friends I attended church with all of those years have since become unchurched. For most of these unchurched friends, the last question speaks to the heart of the matter. As university students, we attended "Convocation," where we saw great concerts and heard some fascinating debates and lectures on a variety of topics. But when we attended chapel on Wednesday nights, we encountered a clique of close-knit Christian friends who weren't certain how to welcome outsiders into their midst. We studied diverse thinkers and challenging writings throughout the week, only to attend Sunday morning worship and hear overly-simplified messages about believing in God and trusting the Bible. We partied hard with loud music and abundant food choices only to return to our home churches for the holidays and partake in polite conversation over sugary Kool-aid or a weak cup of generic coffee. We developed friendships and mentoring relationships with students and professors from around the globe only to see in our church newsletters that there was controversy about sending mission assistance to Communist-controlled third world countries. And when we received tearful phone calls from parents who were divorcing or from siblings who needed to tell the family that they were gay, we received letters from our home churches asking if we wanted to remove our names from the membership roles.

After those exciting college years of exposure to diversity and challenge, church began to seem tame in comparison. We had seen how relevant and meaningful that relationships, learning, and growth could be. When those first years out of college became filled with so many obligatory expenditures of time, we seldom wanted to spend our little bit of free time on irrelevant and meaningless activities. For many of my friends, church had become one of those irrelevant and meaningless activities. Our desire for intellectual stimulation, openness to doubts and questions about life and faith, and our increasing acceptance of diversity did not find fertile ground for further growth in the church. Actually, those desires, open-mindedness, and accepting attitudes were not always considered positive attributes as we returned to the churches of our hometowns. So, it comes as no surprise to me that so many of my previously-churched friends are now "unchurched."

"Unchurched?" you may ask. "How can they be 'unchurched' if they grew up in the church?" Perhaps that very common question is one of the reasons why I do not like to use the term "unchurched" or "churched." When I speak of "unchurched," I simply mean persons who do not have an active, ongoing relationship with a church body. Some of those people may attend for holidays and family gatherings. Others may attend funerals and weddings. Others may never attend as adults, but attended often as children. Some may be experimenting with other spiritual walks of life. But all of these persons are truly Seekers of God, Seekers of God's love, and Seekers of lives that have purpose and meaning.

My "Seeker" friends from college do not lead vacuous lives. Most of them have married and created communities of "family" from a vast array of friends, neighbors, and co-workers. Most of them struggle to keep up with their mortgage and credit card payments while still figuring out a way to keep in touch with one another from hundreds of miles away. Most of my friends are overwhelmed with the time demands of work and family, to the point of constant fatigue and high levels of stress seeming almost normal. And now, most of us are linked a little more inexpensively and a lot more closely through the Internet. For the first time, I have managed to create a web that connects my closest friends from college in Indianapolis with my seminary friends from Boston with my first pastoral colleagues from Detroit with my new-found community of friends in Seattle. We share jokes and bits of advice, hopes and dreams, fears and doubts, encouragement and inspiration across denominational and religious lines without a second thought. My "Seeker" friends seem to have no trouble "getting the punch line" of a church joke, nor do my church friends seem all that offended from the somewhat rude jokes that come across my email.

My passion for Seekers grows with each passing day as more and more of my friends reach stages in life where the questions become more challenging. My interest in reaching Seekers increases with each passing year as I see their desires for community and spiritual guidance become more compelling. The mission and vision for my life and ministry express this interest as it relates to God's call in my life. Yet, when that question comes across my web connection, "So, Mary, I'm thinking about looking for a church, where should I start?" I tremble. When a Seeker wants to join the spiritual journey of the Christian community, where can a Seeker find a warm welcome and a safe space for entry into that community?

This book comes as my invitation to pastors and church leaders around the country and throughout the world to understand my unchurched friends and to recognize the needs of Seekers. We are then better able to respond by creating welcoming environments where Seekers can join the Christian journey and grow as disciples of Jesus Christ.

MISSION

To Share God's Love With All

VISION

To pursue the lost and
share the Good News of God's love,
so that all may know and
accept God's love through Christ
To help persons grow in this faith
so that they may share
God's love with others

SCRIPTURE

Matthew 28:19–20

PASSION

To pursue & connect with the lost, young adults of our country so that they may know and share God's love.

Seekers: Who Are They?

In this book, the term "Seekers" refers to the unchurched people of North America who are seeking spiritual direction and guidance for their lives without affiliation in a religious community. Some books labels these folks as "unchurched," "non-Christian," or "pre-Christian." Whatever the label, Seekers are unchurched only in that they do not currently have an ongoing relationship with a church community. Some may have been raised in the church; others may have never entered a church. Seekers may be young or old, although the percentage of Seekers to active church members is much higher in younger generations than in older generations. Seekers may or may not have church background, but Seekers in North America are seldom ignorant of basic Christian ideas and ideologies. However, for most Seekers, the ideas and ideologies are a confused conglomeration of pop culture's portrayal of the church and the church's public image as presented through television ministries and news media attention.

Contrary to most stereotypes, Seekers have actively pursued theological and spiritual quests long before they enter the doors of a church. Some Seekers spend hours searching for "just the right" Bible or studying any number of religious and spiritual writings. Others pursue their spiritual quest through meditation or conversation with friends. Some have attended Native American ceremonies or channeling sessions, searching for a genuine way to find meaning and purpose in this life.

Most Seekers strive for value-laden lives and a connection with some element of the eternal and the divine in this world. Some Seekers have found this connection in nature or in charitable works. Others hope to find fulfillment in living good lives and praying with their children at bed-time. But when Seekers find that their strivings still leave them feeling empty, they will look for more intense or long-lasting connections with the Holy.

Seekers often read religious books in their spare time, as evidenced by the increasing popularity of "angel" literature. Seekers sometimes even share religious stories with their children and grandchildren. Over and over again, I encounter Seekers who have not set foot in a church for years but have shared Bible stories with their children every week. Other Seekers come into my life who seldom express their faith in public, but can easily debate a well-read Christian in the writings of Augustine or Reinhold Niebuhr. Even popular Christian authors such as Billy Graham, Robert Schuller, and Stephen Lawhead find their ways onto the bookshelves of many Seekers.

It is also erroneous to believe that Seekers are more sinful than most active Christians. As a whole, Seekers are no more lazy or selfish than Christians. On the contrary, Seekers make up a large portion of the volunteer corps and financiers for organizations like The Humane Society, Habitat for Humanity, and Public Television. Seekers are often more able than active churchgoers to share their time in public service, because they are not burdened down with church committee meetings or service requirements to a Christian community. Many Seekers come to the forefront in public debates about ecology, political reform, hunger, children's health, and justice issues. This is particularly noticeable in the entertainment community, where very few "famous names" are active in a church community. Even so, the entertainment community in recent years has become increasingly active in volunteer and service activities locally and globally. On a less famous level, churchgoers would find Seekers in their own community sharing the same compassion and concern for needs very similar to those that concern Christians.

Unlike many active churchgoers, however, Seekers are steeped in the secular world. Seekers are comfortable with the multifaceted messages presented to people through music, television, film, and news. However, Seekers are not any more comfortable than churchgoers with the increasing negativity

18

and de-humanization seen in so many of these messages. Seekers are commonly exposed to the vast amount of violence and sex portrayed through all of these media avenues, even when they are uncomfortable with such graphic imagery. Seekers seldom create a bubble of indifference (as churchgoers sometimes do). Rather, Seekers try to create a balance between being in a world that is troubling and seeking to change this world into something more worthwhile and uplifting. Seekers are often more candid than churchgoers about life's challenges, such as caring for aging parents that annoy them or working for employers they do not respect. Seekers tend to be more honest than churchgoers about the fact that we are all surrounded by, and sometimes even tempted to succumb to, the quick gratification of divorce, violence, drug abuse, addictive behaviors, and dysfunctional relationships.

On the other side of the coin, Seekers are likely to greatly appreciate the freedom of expression present in today's society. Whether the Seeker turns to Rush Limbaugh or MTV for commentaries on current events, the Seeker welcomes the input of outspoken and candid leaders in our society. The vast majority of Seekers enjoy the laughter and irony found on the situation comedies of weeknight television, such as *Friends* or *Home Improvement*. Many are mesmerized by the in-depth exploration of life's grisly side on weeknight realistic and science fiction dramas, such as *NYPD Blue* or *The X-Files*. Seekers are seldom apologetic for the contemporary emphasis on material accumulation and self-sufficiency, and usually strive for those goals in their own lives. In short, Seekers live in the secular world, even as they pursue a spiritual journey. Seekers integrate the experiences of that secular world with the path of a spiritual journey. The challenge for the church is to help Seekers integrate those experiences in a way that leads them to Christ as the guiding light for such integration. In so doing, both Followers and Seekers can begin to dispel the darkness that comes from so much of society's negative and narcissistic tendencies.

Potential Followers

Followers refer to those people who have made an active commitment to accept God's call in their lives and follow the spiritual path where God leads. For Christians, this path comes through the grace of Jesus the Christ and the guidance of the Holy Spirit. Christian Followers may or may not be church members, but they tend to live out their faith commitment through active participation in a worshiping community. Followers may range greatly in their commitment levels, from folks who worship weekly to those who spend almost every night of the week in church or community service.

However, in the church, one cannot assume that all who attend and participate are Followers. Some persons are still exploring possibilities and seeking the Holy One without any level of commitment or assurance in that journey. Other persons are affiliated with churches for any variety of social, professional, or personal reasons that may or may not even bring them to the Seekers' journey. However, we can rest assured that the Holy Spirit is still present when these Seekers or would-be Seekers are present in the Christian worshiping community!

From Matthew 28:19-20
"Go to the people of all nations and make them my disciples. Baptize them . . . and teach them to do everything I have told you." (Contemporary English Version)

All Seekers are potential Followers, for the process of Seeking itself means that a Seeker is willing to find something. And when the discovered item is worth following, you can bet that the Seeker will become a Follower. Thus, the task of Followers becomes that of helping Seekers to find the treasured gift of God's love. The Great Commission in Matthew 28 provides Jesus' compelling call to this mission of helping Seekers (people of all nations) to become Followers (disciples).

A Theology of Unity

Some authors advocate the separation of Seekers from Followers in worship, Bible study, and ministry. The fact is, in each of these settings, Seekers are already in the midst of Followers. Moreover, evidence from the early church indicates that such an integration is fully in line with God's purpose and plan for the church community. In Acts 2, a crowd of Jesus' followers is gathered together. As the Holy Spirit begins filling them and the noise of the diverse languages begins to fill the streets of Jerusalem, unconverted Jews apparently joined the crowd. Peter began preaching—to Seekers and Followers—as the corporate worship experience continued. No one seemed concern on that exciting day of Pentecost whether Seekers were separate from Followers.

Similarly, in Acts 16, Paul and Silas begin worshiping God in the jail, singing and praying aloud for all to hear. In that public act of worship, right in the midst of criminals and a Roman jailer, Paul and Silas shared God's word. The jailer turned from Seeker to Follower because of his interaction with Paul and Silas, and his admiration for their great faith. Had they not shared their faith through public worship in the midst of Seekers, the jailer might never have seen God's grace in action.

Theologically, I refuse to believe that God has issued a separation of the sacred from the secular in this world. And yet, the church lives as if God had done just that. Whereas God has created a world of wholeness and completeness (Gen. 1:31–2:2), the church often prefers categories and divisions. Whereas Christ has promised that his Body on earth is to be

21

unified and cooperative (Ephesians. 4:4–13), the church often seems content with a Body that is lopsided and missing several organs or limbs. To invite Seekers into the church, the church can create an environment where the sacred and the secular are integrated. To welcome Seekers into the Body of Christ, we must be prepared for the Body to be whole and complete, with all of the diversity and complexity that such wholeness will bring. To minister with Seekers, we begin to see Seekers as "us" rather than "them." Seeker and Pop singer Joan Osborne sings the words, "What if God was one of us?" What indeed. The parable of the goats and the sheep comes to mind. Osborne's words echo this parable's stern warning that what we have done to the least (or the "other") we have done to Christ (Matthew 25:32–46). In churches today, the Seeker too often becomes the one who is refused food and drink, clothing and ministry, warmth and hospitality. Church leaders risk hearing one day that we are now fated with the goats of that parable for our unwillingness to see "them" as "us." Even when we are not able to see the Seeker as "one of us" or "Christ in disguise," we can remember that sheep-Followers are not the judges. In the mean time, we are called to respond with love and care to all whom we meet. For Seekers, that love and care needs to take the form of welcome and acceptance as Seekers join Followers on the spiritual journey of life.

One of the challenges in opening the church's ministries to Seekers is the tendency to believe that the church's goal of excellence, or its veneer of theological correctness, will somehow be threatened. Sometimes, the theological doubts of Followers may come to light more clearly when Seekers openly express doubts and questions. Sometimes, the "perfect" behavior and clean-cut appearances of churchgoers may be overshadowed by Seekers who leave worship early or wear casual clothes. Even the church's morality and value systems may feel a bit threatened when Seekers ask questions about those "gray areas" that Followers haven't found adequate answers for in their own lives. Still, Christ's Gospel teaches clearly and completely that excellence is meaningless unless accompanied by an excellent ("pure") heart (Matthew 19:16–26; Matthew 15:8–12).

Jesus himself often argued with the Scribes and Pharisees about this temptation to worry more about pure appearances than pure motives. For instance, in Mark 3:1-5, Jesus chose to heal on the Sabbath day. Such work was clearly forbidden by the religious laws he had agreed to obey as a Jewish man. In meeting the need of someone in pain instead of obeying a law that he knew well, Jesus taught that theological correctness is never an excuse to ignore an opportunity for ministry.

When I encounter musicians who cannot tolerate the use of pop music in a worship service, I encourage them to use their excellent training to create pop music of the highest quality for the glory of God. In working with preachers who are offended when I suggest an illustration from a recent Hollywood movie, I remind them to re-read the Gospel of their choice. All four Gospels make this point quite clearly: The good news of God's unconditional love is to be proclaimed widely and loudly, so that all people have the opportunity to become disciples of Jesus Christ. No "law" of our religious institutions is supposed to impede that proclamation, and when it does we risk becoming preservers of a dead heritage. Thus, ministry with Seekers will often mean incorporating secular media and music into the church's life and worship. Such unity of sacred and secular represents the unity that Christ offers to saints and sinners alike. Together, we are all given the opportunity to experience God's love through the grace of Christ's gift on the cross.

The Spiritual Needs of Seekers

Above all else, most Seekers are in need of community, the type of community where God's love is expressed freely and unconditionally. Most Seekers in our society today are part of the transience that will symbolize American life for at least the early part of the next century. Many Seekers are of the younger generations who will be the most profoundly impacted by the shrinking size of our world and the increasing size of corporations. Seekers are currently on a lonely spiritual journey, perhaps with only the companionship of a spouse or a friend. When a Seeker enters the church, the Seeker is exploring the possibility of expanding that spiritual journey into a community experience.

In order for the church to address this communal need of Seekers, the church faces the opportunity of living its faith as a Body of Christ. In the earliest days of the church's birth, the need for community was always recognized and church leaders insisted that community needs be prioritized above individual needs. Immediately after the dramatic birth of the church on Pentecost, Acts 2:42–47 records that meeting regularly and sharing everything had become cornerstones of the early church's life together. Throughout the letters of the New Testament, early church leaders are advising Followers to live out this unity of purpose and communal caring for one another. Many of the letters seem to be primarily directed at helping young churches learn how to live in community more lovingly and more effectively.

In the American church, we have lost much of that heritage. Seekers can help us re-claim that part of our heritage, helping both Followers and Seekers to find the support and fulfillment that community can provide. In re-claiming that heritage, the church will again be capable of serving and following Christ more effectively as well. The value placed on self-sufficiency threatens many churches and many Christians today. In individuals, this can be seen in the desire for death when a person needs assistance from others because of medical limitations. In churches, this value of self-sufficiency is exemplified when churchgoers prefer to close a church rather than build a stronger community by welcoming new persons into the church. Such self-sufficiency is neither a solid Christian value, nor an intention that early church leaders had for the church's existence. Seekers who begin investigating the church seem to know this inherently. Thus, when Seekers sniff out a church whose desire for self-sufficiency is higher than its desire for ministry, Seekers will turn away. However, when Seekers find a church whose passion for ministry is intertwined with its commitment to community, Seekers will often choose that church as a place to further grow on the spiritual journey.

Likewise, Seekers are seldom interested in preserving a dead heritage. In many ways, the spiritual needs of Seekers can revitalize local churches because of the openness of that spiritual pursuit. Seekers do not enter church doors looking to preserve the role of the Church Council or protect the pension plan of the pastor. Seekers enter church doors to find a community that will help in the pursuit of a spiritual journey.

In order for the church to be such a community, the church must itself be on a spiritual journey. The church needs a vision of itself as a community of persons seeking God and growing in love of God and neighbor. Unless a church can see itself in this way, all of the programs and plans in the world will not develop a successful ministry with Seekers. Seekers, like most Followers, do not need more obligatory meetings or scheduled events in their lives. Rather, both Seekers and Followers need gatherings and opportunities to grow in relationship to God and the world. This growth happens when the church is fulfilling Christ's mission of sharing God's message of love and grace here on earth.

Again, when Seekers suspect that a church is simply a conglomeration of programs, committees, meetings, and small groups that have little purpose other than simply filling the church calendar, Seekers will abandon that church. But when Seekers recognize a community that is striving to grow together in Christ, to learn more about its faith, and to struggle with the ways of living out that faith, Seekers will respond positively to that community. In many ways, searching for Seekers can help the church to live its mission more faithfully than in the past. Seekers' yearning for genuine spirituality and dedicated growth on the spiritual journey can become contagious in a community of Followers and Seekers. As that yearning spreads through a community of faith, the church will find itself living out Christ's mission fervently. Indeed, the church has always been at its best when it has had to examine itself and re-claim that focus on living the Christian mission. Seekers will insist on such an examination if churches strive to find and welcome Seekers together with Followers onto the Christian journey.

Although Seekers will have been on spiritual journeys long before entering church doors, Seekers often come to the church when that need for spiritual nourishment can no longer be met in isolation. Previously for Seekers, spiritual nourishment may have meant private meditation, nature walks, or quiet reading. As Seekers enter the church community, that spiritual nourishment may take the form of prayer support, small group study, relevant biblical preaching, and uplifting worship experiences. Spiritual nourishment provides the sustenance that a Seeker needs to survive in a world of isolation, selfishness, hatred, and negativity. For such is the world that we encounter when we open ourselves to the secular values that pervade our society.

However, Seekers also come to church in a desire for open and honest theological exchange. Seekers welcome the opportunity for theological challenge. In the theological struggle, Seekers find that doubts are countered with belief, and questions are often answered as new questions emerge. As a Seeker-Follower, I am comfortable living "in the questions" and I prefer to allow churchgoers to do the same. Mainline churches in the liberal tradition have many gifts to offer Seekers: a theological heritage of dialogue and discussion, an openness to diversity and pluralism, and an acceptance of questions and doubts. In so many of the faith traditions that strive to reach Seekers, faith is seen as "finding the right answers in order to live the right way." For Seekers, this can be an offensive means of exploring spirituality. However, many faith traditions have a very different understanding of faith than simply a path to the "right answers." In this latter group, faith is seen as a process or a journey. Faith becomes an opportunity to grow in one's understanding of God, one's love of God and neighbor, and one's personhood and servanthood as a Follower of God. In these traditions, Seekers can find the room needed to explore faith questions, live with nagging doubts, and grow through those same experiences of questioning and doubting. Seekers need a safe place where these questions and doubts can be explored. Seldom does a Seeker come to a church seeking the outrageous moralist condemnation of Dr. Laura. Nor is a Seeker likely to enter a church in search of the wavering belief system of so many politicians. Rather, a Seeker comes to church in hope of asking the questions, exploring the doubts, and finding the answers necessary to integrate the spiritual journey with the challenging life events we face regularly. When Seekers encounter churches that seem to have all the answers, most Seekers will suspect a lack of authenticity and honesty. In contrast, when Seekers encounter churches that are willing to wrestle with the questions, Seekers will likely respond by sharing their own struggles. This does not mean that Seekers want undeveloped theologies or relativistic doctrines in churches. Seekers understand that one can hold a belief strongly while still exploring the problems inherent in that belief. Seekers (and Followers) also need the room to accept or reject various church doctrines during the spiritual growth process. Quite frankly, Followers who can acknowledge that we are still Seekers in terms of struggling, questioning, and growing will become welcoming and caring friends for Seekers who want to know more about following God.

Finally, Seekers need a relevant reason for turning to Christ. On this spiritual journey, Seekers may or may not have encountered Christ. So when a Seeker comes to church, that Seeker is likely looking for what it is that Christians have that would be helpful on the Seeker's spiritual journey. For that reason, I always encourage churchgoers to be honest about their Christianity in life outside of church. For when a Seeker encounters a Christian who lives a little less selfishly and a little more kindly than other people in the same environment, the Seeker often begins to ponder the Christian influence. "What do they have that I don't?" When a Seeker receives helpful care or guidance from a Christian who neither judges nor ignores their faith differences, the Seeker is given a glimpse into the Christ-message that Jesus brought during his walk on this earth. Seekers come to church looking for that glimpse. And when that glimpse shows a relevant difference that Christ can provide for the lives of Followers, the Seeker is likely to join on the Christian spiritual journey.

These are some of the basic spiritual needs of the Seekers that I encounter. The needs are not all that different from the basic spiritual needs of most Followers of Christ. Yet, these needs are so seldom truly met in the church.

SEEKERS LOOK FOR:

Community

Spiritual Nourishment

Theological Challenge

Safe Places to Explore Questions & Doubts

A Relevant Message of Good News

A Reason for Turning to Christ

The Call to Search for Seekers

Shortly after I drafted the proposal for this book, I recognized that a passion had begun to grow in my soul. Until I went on retreat one day in 1996, I could not clarify why this book seemed so important to me. However, on retreat, I developed my personal mission and vision statements and realized that this book was an outgrowth of my particular call to proclaim the Gospel. In order to share God's love with all people as a Christian minister, I feel called to assist churches in becoming places where Seekers as well as Followers can feel welcome. Followers and church leaders need to recognize the close relationship between Seekers and Followers, and the sincere spiritual needs and interests of Seekers.

The spiritual yearning of Seekers seems obvious, but perhaps Followers are confused by the low interest level of Seekers regarding the church. Indeed, the low participation level in organized religion does not seem to indicate an increased level of spiritual passion in our society. However, as we look at the ways in which people respond to spiritual topics outside of the church, we begin to see how prevalent spiritual yearning actually is. Such yearning is seen in the success of movies like *Ghost, Michael,* and *The Preacher's Wife,* where theological questions about angels, morality, community, love, reincarnation, and death are explored. In book stores across the country, the increased literary interest in angels points to the human desire for contact with the divine. And the religious ponderings of contemporary song writers in songs like "Losing My Religion" by R.E.M., "Oh, Father" by Madonna, and "Counting Blue Cars" ("Tell Me All Your Thoughts on God") by Dishwalla should make religious leaders in all faith traditions take notice. The spiritual explorations of today's pop artists preclude any sanguine denial by Followers that unchurched society is spiritually bankrupt. On the contrary, some of the most honest discussions of theological questions and pursuits of spiritual integrity are happening outside the walls of the church. The continued growth of non-traditional religions across North America is no longer simply a remnant of the "flower child" movement from the 1960s and 1970s. People of all ages are searching for gurus, turning to New Age centers and bookstores, consulting spiritualists or astrologers in decision-making, or looking for therapists who can provide spiritual direction in conjunction with more traditional psychological guidance. Unchurched people show up in downtown Seattle during the lunch time Taize' service and at the late night Episcopal Service of Compline; they visit the labyrinth of meditation and reflection in the nearby suburbs; others pack the KingDome and other stadiums across the country to attend Promise Keepers' rallies. What is all this about if not a spiritual yearning?

Yet, church leaders continue to excuse the lack of outreach to Seekers on the argument that unchurched people won't respond to the church's overtures to join the Christian journey. It becomes easy for church leaders to accuse Seekers of shallow commitment, low initiative, degenerating value systems, obsession with careers, and rejection of tradition. The truth, however, may be far different. I see Seekers who ignore the church because of the church's lack of communication to the outside world. Seekers sense the church's ambivalence about inviting newcomers and the lack of value the church places on Seekers. Seekers far too often also recognize the church's obsession with its own needs. The church's sheer busy-ness can become a stumbling block for Seekers. Moreover, the church's desire to shield its programs and traditions from change are discerned by Seekers as red flags that Seekers are not really welcome. Thus, many people who are actively pursuing a spiritual journey are not turning to the church for nourishment, challenge, growth, or relevance.

Yet, no organization is better-able to help persons who are seeking God than the Church that Jesus Christ gave birth to through the Holy Spirit. Christ created the Church for the very purpose of reaching Seekers, that Seekers might become Followers who walk with Christ on the journey (Acts 2:41). Christ created the Church so that all Believers might go out and make Followers of all Seekers (Matthew 28:19–20).

And no place in the Church is better able to welcome Seekers into the Christian journey, in a non-threatening and invitational way, than the worship life of the Church. Because worship brings the human creation together with the divine, the sacred and the secular are unified in the worship experience. Worship is that place where we intentionally invite the sacred into our secular existence. Worship is the time when our secular lives are merged with the sacred life of God in the most profound manner. This is not simply a time to exalt the Holy, but also a time and space to experience or simply observe the Holy. Worship with an attitude of praise, hope, strength, and courage begins to dispel the loneliness and isolation that arise when we find ourselves feeling separate and distant from God.

Once we recognize that fact, it is a small step to the realization that Seekers and Followers are equally capable and deserving of entering into that holy time called worship. Together, we all can enjoy the opportunity to give praise, honor, glory, and power to God. I find it terribly troubling that so much of the Christian literature about the unchurched in the last 20 years asserts that Seekers are incapable and undeserving of the worship of God. Time and again, Jesus emphasized that no person had the right to deny another access to God (see John 8:7 as one example). Likewise, the Book of Hebrews reminds us that Jesus alone lived without sin (4:15–16); the rest of us need all the help we can get from our worshiping communities to lead godly lives. Through God's gift of grace in Christ, we are all—saint or sinner—invited to approach God's throne of mercy. Because of the inherent divine image present in every human being (Genesis 1:26–27)—Christian or not—we can trust that God is present and available to Seekers and Followers alike. Surely, there is no better place for Followers to invite Seekers into God's presence than in the worship setting itself.

Worship can reflect the faith journey of both Followers and Seekers, so that faith is ignited or renewed. Worship can also reflect the mission of the church, as the church seeks to be a reconciler and a mediator between the real world we live in, and the ideal world we strive for (God's realm or kingdom). As the church seeks to be an instrument of both consensus or peace and prophecy or challenge, worship provides some semblance of God's realm here and now. In doing so, worship

31

affirms the worth of all persons, striving for partnership in spiritual growth and missional outreach to all of humanity. In this way, worship provides a foundation of faith.

Worship reflects these journeys of faith and mission by being incarnational. In worship, persons experience the risen Christ and are encouraged to be transformed by Christ's presence in the world because of that worship experience. In worship, we experience both the presence and transcendence of God, as we feel God as close to us as our own breath while recognizing that God often remains as distant as the farthest star. As Followers worship God, much of the self-centeredness that separates us from God is overcome by the very presence of the sacred entering our secular existence. As Seekers enter this setting, Seekers may encounter God directly or may simply observe the interaction between Followers and God. In either case, the Seeker has encountered the intersection of the sacred and the secular in moments of grace. Truly, life is never the same after we encounter such moments. Worship provides the opportunity to fulfill one of the most precious responsibilities Christians have to share the good news of following Christ with those who are seeking.

This is not to say that merging the sacred and the secular in the worship setting is an easy task. Nor is the merging of Seekers and Followers into one community a simple step for churches to take. However, in this joining of secular to sacred, Seeker to Follower, we are shown the possibility of embracing and sharing God's love in ways that Christ intended. Indeed, this intersection of Seekers and Followers, sacred and secular, is a wonderful opportunity for living out Christ's presence in the life of the church.

In this book, we will explore ways of uniting the sacred and the secular so that Seekers are invited and feel welcomed into the Christian community. If we open our hearts, open our minds, and allow the Holy Spirit to guide our learning, we will find that Seekers are ready to join us on the journey to Christian maturity together.

CHAPTER TWO

Generation to Generation

Although the percentage of Seekers to Followers seems to be exploding in the younger generations of our country, Seekers have always been a part of Christian life. When I was a youth pastor, I confirmed a young woman whose parents had never attended church until her confirmation day. At the reception following the service, her father made a point of thanking me for my influence in Michelle's life. I was a bit amazed at his warmth, since Michelle had always confessed her embarrassment that her parents were atheists. Tellingly, her father told me, "You know, we all believe the same thing here. God is what it's all about. I just express it a little differently than you church folks do."

Seekers are not as unfamiliar to Followers as you might think. Even portrayed in movies and television shows, Seekers are actually well known to most people. During my childhood, Daddy Walton represented a similar attitude. In the 1970s' family drama *The Waltons,* everyone else went to church weekly. However, the father preferred to spend his time in his wood shop, in the forest, or on the mountain. In any of these places, he found ways of seeking and finding God. Often, his theological ponderings were the most profound of anyone's in the family. A bumper sticker I saw recently summed this up perfectly: "I'd rather be in the mountains thinking about God, than in church thinking about the mountains."

The existence of Seekers is nothing new in American life. However, the increasing number of Seekers and decreasing number of Followers has forced an issue that most churches have not faced in the 20th century: how to reach Seekers and help them to become Followers.. In order to do this effectively, church leaders need to understand the diversity amongst Seekers. One means of understanding Seekers is to understand the generations from which they come and the issues and attitudes that help define and shape these generations.

On any given Sunday morning across North America, Seekers and Followers of every generation are present in Christian worship. Some attend for the sake of children and grandchildren; others attend at the request of parents or spouses. Some attend because of business or work-related connections; others attend out of tradition and habit. Some attend because of their friendships within the church; others attend because of their obligations within the church. And on any given Sunday morning, many people also attend because they are seeking spiritual nourishment.

Ironically, on any given Sunday morning across America, there are Seekers and Followers who stay home for the exact same reasons. They stay home to spend quality time with children or grandchildren, to care for parents or to please a spouse. Others choose to use Sundays to catch up on work assignments or to get dressed and go to work. Still others follow their Sunday traditions of catching up on sleep and reading the paper, spending time with friends, or catching up on other obligations in the community. Those who believe that the church offers Seekers an excellent place to explore and deepen their spiritual lives face a disheartening fact: Many people intentionally stay away from organized worship on Sunday morning in order to seek spiritual nourishment through other means.

These statements hold true across generational lines. Despite stereotypes to the contrary, there has never been a time in North American history when the herd mentality was so strong that everyone dutifully got in their car on Sunday morning to go to church. In each generation, we find persons

who attend church and persons who do not. But before exploring this fact more deeply, an overview of the current understanding of different American generations will prove useful.

FOLLOWERS AND SEEKERS ARE PRESENT IN EVERY GENERATION

Builders — (born 1901–1924) The civic generation that builds and protects

Balancers — (born 1925–1942) The silent generation that balances and mediates the excesses of the building and booming generations

Boomers — (born 1943–1960) The movers & shakers who are instruments of change

Busters — (born 1961–1981) The "X"generation that busts stereotypes as it reacts to change

Birthers — (born 1982–???) A new civic generation predicted to rebuild institutions and values lost in the last few generations[1]

The Builders

Generational theories have been receiving increased attention since Strauss and Howe published their seminal work, *Generations*. This book explores the repetitive pattern of generational history throughout the American experience. For the purposes of reaching Seekers at the turn of the 20th century, we can confine our interest to the generations currently living in North America. Our eldest Seekers are part of the generation (born 1901–1924) who lived through both World Wars and helped to rebuild our world following each of those wars. These Seekers are part of a civic generation that put its trust in institutions and organizations. This generation, often referred to as the GI generation, is aging quickly but is still very invested in the organizations it built and preserved. People of this generation often find it hard to relate to younger generations who seem cynical and ambivalent about such institutions. On the other hand, many people in this generation are suffering as their beloved institutions abandon them or begin dying from lack of support amongst the younger generations. Within the church, this generation is filled with people who are highly committed to the church and its ministry, and will give all that they have in order to help the church survive and grow. I refer to these persons as Builders.

The Balancers

The Builders gave birth to the generation that grew up during World War II. This generation, sometimes called the Silent Generation (born 1925–1942), has had to adapt to the changing world their parents created. This generation carried us through the Cold War, somehow balancing the power and strength of two large countries with the fears and weaknesses of political leaders and citizens that threatened to destroy the world. I call the people of this generation the Balancers. Not only have they helped to balance a country through many decades of turmoil, but they have had to mediate the differences between their parents and their children. This generation is often accused of sitting on the fence. For instance, they have never elected a President from their own generation. However, experience teaches that they sit on fences only in the hope of caring for the generations thta surround them. Balancers are often ambivalent about the current state of the church, wondering whether it shouldn't be more like the church they grew up in or more like the "modern" church they read about in newspapers and magazines. Within the local church, Balancers are often quiet members of committees who help to release deadlocks that threaten to halt new ministries. Balancers, although not as self-sacrificial as their parents, are committed to giving of themselves and their gifts to the church and other institutions that they have helped to preserve during their balancing-act lives. Some Balancers are puzzled by the lack of a similar commitment amongst younger Followers, while other Balancers excuse their children's lack of commitment because of increasing costs and demands on their children's lives. In both cases, Balancers are well-versed in the concept of guilt, and their own investment in guilt-motivated giving can be a strength and a hindrance to the church. In the church, Balancers who find ways of balancing their own guilt-motivated giving with a sense of God's liberating grace are more likely to relate effectively to younger generations. These Balancers are also more likely to enjoy the fruits of their labor and commitment as they age and slow down in their commitment level.

The Boomers

The famous Baby Boomers (born 1943–1960) are known for their idealism about the world and their rejection of traditional institutions and organizations. Even so, they have become movers and shakers within those very institutions, often doing so with attempts to serve as the instruments of change.

In churches, these Boomers are rising into leadership positions and trying to find ways to offer their ideals and dreams of change while preserving certain traditions they have become equally idealistic about preserving. Boomers offer an interesting mix of progressive thinking and reactionary road-blocking in the church. As they reach mid-life, Boomers experience the need for stability and peace that most mid-lifers have experienced throughout the generations. Likewise, Boomers sometimes find themselves very invested in preserving whatever "new and radical" institutions they have created or whatever "old and traditional" institutions they have chosen to preserve. In either case, Boomers can appear a bit like Builders when Boomers are committed to a cause. But, Boomers may fight to the death to deny such a claim, knowing that similar attitudes of the Builders made the Boomers' younger years frightening and frustrating. Even as Boomers grow in their levels of responsibility and power, they are realizing that the volunteer and financial power of their generation will never equal that of the previous two generations. Thus, they often look to their parents (the Balancers) to support their efforts. This is particularly true for Boomers who have invested their lives in charitable and community organizations. Interestingly, many of these Boomers are giving birth to the next generation of Builders (the Birthers, born 1982 - ???) who are likely to drive them as crazy as does the previous generation of Builders.

The Busters

Born approximately 1961–1981 is that elusive generation that refuses to be labeled. The thirteenth generation born in America, this "X" or "13er" Generation is considered by Boomers to be a "lost generation" and is known for its reactive attitude toward Boomers and its alienated situation in American society. I call the people of this generation Busters. This generation will bust all previous glass ceilings, not because they will have great success in the traditional marketplace but because they exhibit an independence and an entrepreneurial spirit that defies even the most aggressive of Boomers. Even so, this is likely to be one of the poorest generations in American history. Many Busters will be poor not in the sense of dollars and cents, but in the sense of spending power compared with the generations surrounding them. The chasm between rich and poor will be the widest in this generation, and it is yet to be seen how this generation will cope with this discrepancy of wealth and affluence in their friendships and communities. This is a generation of workers who must react to the changes (and conflicts) that Boomers, Balancers, and Builders have brought to American life. Often, such reaction includes busting the values placed on the traditional American work ethic and the prejudices that continue to divide Americans.

Busters are not interested in "programs" of inclusiveness; they prefer to simply "walk the talk" and create the diversity of friendships that their older sibling and parents speak so eloquently about. Of course, some Busters are also reacting to the Boomers' idealism by lapsing into age-old prejudices based on race and ethnic origin. Even within these seemingly homogenous "hate groups," a perceptive researcher discovers great diversity. Within a single gang or group of Busters, individuals from all ends of the economic and class spectrum may gather to look for community in a world of isolation.

This generation will bustle with energy, cleaning up the messes created by the "me" attitudes of the 1970s and the devastation created by 30 years of Cold War. The selfish attitudes of corporate America and young entrepreneurs 30 years ago have led to excessive environmental problems. The value placed on self-satisfaction during the sexual revolution has led to a dramatic rise in sexually transmitted diseases, teen pregnancies, and abortion rates at all age levels. As Busters see it, the idealistic political and social stances of the Boomers have led to increased violence and upheaval in the American political scene. For now, the "clean-up" is taking place in grass roots efforts toward recycling and environmental concern (without turning to federal environmental agencies for protection). Young Busters have not adequately addressed the alarming difficulties arising out of the sexual revolution, but I suspect that they will as they mature. On the political scene, Busters are attempting their own "clean-up" of the political system by supporting independent and maverick-style candidates. Globally, this generation is more likely to respond to economic and political disasters with hands-on efforts. Small relief organizations are sending Busters to countries like Bosnia where one-on-one relief efforts and friendship-missions have an immediate impact on the lives of individuals, and perhaps on the greater political struggle.

Busters are bustling with energy as they "clean up" the technological mess of a generation of uncoordinated technology races. Busters pride themselves in finding ways to integrate previously incompatible computer systems, hacking into in-communicative Internet sites, and connecting technology tools like compact disc players, computers, and telephones into compatible units. Busters are seldom interested in the "rules" of competition and copyrights that would have previously prohibited such integration. Of course, Busters have grown up in the years of de-regulation. This breakdown of institutionalism has surely had its impact on Busters' attitudes toward territorialism and monopolies.

In the church, Busters seem to be a "missing generation." Yet, the careful observer will see Busters present. Often, older Busters (in their late 20s & early 30s) are incorrectly labeled as young Baby Boomers. Younger Busters (young 20s and late teens) tend to be considered children and find difficulty in being taken seriously in the church. Nevertheless, Busters who are present in the church are often highly committed to the church. Busters in the church are often fast-paced in their desire to bring the church into the 21st century, and equally invested in preserving certain traditions of the church in which they were raised.

The Birthers

Finally, we come to the latest generation of Americans, the generation I call the Birthers. Born first in 1982 and predicted to include children born through the year 2003, this millennium generation is likely to be another Builder generation. Children in this generation will likely be raised by parents who instill confidence and determination in these youngsters. Media portrayal of these children will further instill a sense of strength and power to this generation. Although the violence of this generation is prevalently noted in the news at this point in their lives, there is also a self-confidence and strong integrity to this generation. It is likely that we will see that confident strength of the civic leaders and institution builders of this generation surfacing in their late teenage years. This generation of Seekers is likely to be the most highly unchurched group of young Americans in our history. Yet, they are the very ones who will be vested with the responsibility of rebuilding institutions and organizations in their adult years. This is a crucial point for church leaders to recognize, since Birthers will have to decide whether or not the church is worth rebuilding and preserving in their adulthood. This generation will have to re-create much of what we will have lost by the time they are adults, not only in the church but throughout American society. Generational theorists predict that another world crisis in the early 21st century will propel this generation to leadership, a role that these confident children of Boomers and Busters will likely relish.

The Seekers

Although each of these generations is represented in the American church, the youngest generations (Busters and Birthers) represent the greatest numbers of unchurched Seekers. In the Buster generation, there are fruitful opportunities for reaching Seekers since so many young adults in this generation

41

are Seekers. Although this generation represents the highest percentage of unchurched persons in American history (70 percent), this same generation also claims a high percentage of persons who label themselves as Christian (70 percent as well). Unfortunately, when you combine the high percentage of unchurched Busters with the mixed success the church has had in reaching the Boomer generation on any permanent basis, an alarming prediction emerges. It is not unreasonable to predict a 90 percent rate of unchurched persons in the Birther generation (children of Busters and Boomers). Historically, the fact remains that most people make a commitment to Christ before age 18. Of those people, many have had some parental connection to the church. For Birthers, both the parental and the peer connections to the church will be largely absent.

If you are working in a retirement community or one of the many churches across America located in an aging neighborhood, you may be thinking, "Phew! I'm off the hook with these Seekers." Not so fast! Even in the hey-days of the late 1950s, almost half of Americans were somewhere other than worship on Sunday mornings. The number of Americans absent from worship has only increased since then—a statistic not attributable to the younger generations alone. Many young people are unchurched because their parents and grandparents have never connected them with the church. For many young people, the first word they hear about Christ comes from another young person through an evangelical, para-church organization like Youth for Christ or Promise Keepers.

Across the generations, Seekers are turning elsewhere for spiritual fulfillment. Even amongst the mature generational persons who have spent much of lives attending church, church involvement may decrease in later years. Older Seekers may have drifted away from church when they moved to a retirement community or into the homes of their adult children. Reconnecting with a new community of faith is very difficult in those circumstances. Yet, there is probably no time in life when community is more essential than in the golden years of wisdom, reflection, and maturing faith development. Many Builder Seekers left the church after a doctrinal or political dispute with the pastor or church board. Their yearning for a safe space is just as genuine and desperate as that of any younger Seeker. Amongst both Builder and Balancer couples who have always been active in the church, church activity has often been important only to one partner. During the years of widowhood, the other partner is very likely to drift away. In some cases, Balancers have given up on the church because of its inability to reach their Boomer children. When looking at older Seekers, it would be a mistake to assume that all Builders and Balancers have had experience in the church and have simply drifted away through a changing life situation. Recently, one of the Builders in my church started talking with me about his evangelism efforts on the golf course. Despite my recognition that Seekers exist in every generation, I was amazed to hear that every single one of his golf partners (all Builders and Balancers) had been unchurched for most of their lives! Many Seekers of these generations came from highly educated homes in a day when church and science collided, and many thinking persons rejected the church completely. Seekers in these generations may not even realize the amazing progress that the church has made in integrating scientific knowledge into its theological understanding, nor the ways in which the scientific world has become increasingly appreciative of the "unknowns" that religion has insisted upon for decades. Many Builder and Balancer Seekers are of the "Daddy Walton" type, worshipping God in their own way but not too interested in the church's dogmatic ways of trying to confine God in a four-walled, white building. If you are working with an older community, look outside of those white walls and you are likely to find many Seekers waiting for a word of new hope within the church. You will find Seekers who are interested in wrestling with some of life's most challenging and interesting questions: Who am I? Why was I put on this earth? What will I leave behind? What does death mean? What is God? What does God have to do with me? These questions bring to churches a maturity and wisdom that only comes with age and experience. Builder-Seekers are in need of communities of faith where these questions and struggles can be explored and discussed. Likewise, churches are in need of mature questions and struggles like these to guide younger Christians into a more mature faith walk.

The children and grandchildren of these generations can often serve as the best evangelists to Builders, but only when they are in the church. So, what continues to keep Boomers and their children as Seekers only, instead of Followers? Boomers, of course, represent a vast array of viewpoints and ideologies. But, on the whole, the church has missed the Boomers who have remained liberal, even in the "conservative 1980s." This sub-culture of Boomers is highly unchurched, finding communities of faith in close-knit groups of friends and extended family connections. Liberal Boomers' ideal of caring for the earth often collides with church teaching that humans have dominion over the earth. The Boomer ideal of creating an unprejudiced society often collides with the church's attitude that prejudice is something to be overcome gradually so that we don't offend anyone. Some of these same Boomers have been hurt terribly by actions (or lack thereof) on the church's part. Boomers have known a frighteningly high percentage of clergy abuse—both sexual molestation of children and sexual harassment and abuse of adults. Boomers have known theological abuse, when the churches that reached out first and strongest to them were cults and radically conservative churches where judgmentalism and doctrinal purity were paramount, regardless of the price it exacted. Even the Boomers raised in the best parochial schools were often subjected to incredibly strict discipline and seemingly irrelevant theological teachings.

Other Boomers are truly too busy for the church's demands. These Boomers, who are so often portrayed in the media, can hardly fathom giving up their only day off all week

44

(Sunday) for an hour of worship. The thought of giving additional volunteer time or money to the church is overwhelming for people whose lives are spinning out of control with 60-hour work weeks and children who need day planners to keep track of their own activities. I suspect we have never seen a generation of children busier than the children of Boomers, and their busy schedules impose increased scheduling problems on their parents. Of course, many churches have attracted Boomers and their children by simply offering attractive options of programmed events in the church. In doing so, Boomers can continue their hectic lifestyle. They merely do it in a "Christian" setting.

Despite Boomers' many reasons for remaining unchurched, Boomers have intense spiritual needs and probing theological questions to address as we move into the 21st century. What impact has my idealism had? Have I made any difference in this world? Where is God in the midst of my busy life? How can I find some sanity in my busy life? Why do I need God when I am so self-sufficient? Who will my children become in this new century? Who am I as an aging parent? How do I care for my aging parents? Will I die alone? What was this life for anyway? These questions are in need of answers, discussions, and study. The answers Boomer-Seekers will find may not be terribly satisfactory if the church does not find a way to invite Boomer-Seekers into theological dialogue. This maturing population has much to offer and to gain from the Christian spiritual journey, if only the church can find a way to connect meaningfully with Seekers of this generation.

The Buster generation, freer to separate from the Church at an earlier age, seems to have had fewer negative experiences with the church. Most often, this generation has experienced the church as irrelevant and out-of-touch. Those of this generation who have had meaningful experiences in the church are unlikely to turn their backs on the church as long as the church continues to be relevant to their experience. However, a change of pastor or a move to a new state after college is often all it takes for a Buster to drift away from Follower to Seeker. Regrettably, many of the churched children in this generation were raised in churches where children were truly seen and not heard. In the 1970s, a new trend emerged in American churches: Sunday School became a substitute for worship. Children no longer attended worship with their parents; rather, they attended Sunday School with their friends. Then, a funny thing happened when they and their friends reached the adolescent years: Sunday School became irrelevant and worship was boring, so they started sleeping in late on Sunday mornings. Even when Mom or Dad dragged them to church, it was all too obvious to them that other church members were not comfortable with the presence of teenagers in worship. I suppose older generations had reason to be comfortable. Only 10 years before, Boomer teenagers represented the potential overturn of the entire American way of thinking! The disappointing surprise has been the way in which Boomers have grown uncomfortable with the same teenage behaviors that Boomers fought so hard to have accepted during their teenage years.

In one church I served, I discovered that many of the adult Boomers who had enjoyed their own freedom and rebellion as teenagers now insisted on keeping "those teenagers" of the Buster and Birther generations in the youth room during worship services. When we moved Sunday School time so that children and teenagers could attend worship, the back rows of teenagers became one of the most participatory and attentive group of worshippers in the church. Still, their tattered jeans and tight mini-skirts became the controversial focus of many church discussions. Nevertheless, Builders and Balancers became the advocates for these teenagers, saying to the Boomers, "Well, at least these kids value church and listen to the pastor!" Unfortunately, many Busters did not have advocates in their local churches. Even the Busters who have fond memories of Vacation Bible School and Sunday evening youth group are often at a loss to think of one good memory of Sunday morning worship. When I remember my most outstanding childhood worship experience, I remember participating in a children's sermon. After raising my hand to volunteer, I found myself drinking a sip of vinegar while my friend drank a sip of water! To this day, I do not know what the point of that children's message was. I do know that I was unpleasantly surprised at the terrible taste in my mouth. I was also dreadfully embarrassed about the fact that I spit the vinegar back into the cup in front of the entire congregation. Worship memories like this one are not likely to bring Busters back to church!

Other Busters have attended worship only on Christmas or Easter, or for a funeral or wedding. They know that the church exists, and some even wonder why their churched friends never invite them to church. And yet, many churched Busters are hesitant to offer an invitation to their friends when they know that there is not much being offered in the church that will be helpful or relevant to their friends. Busters tend to focus their spiritual needs on creating friendship networks of love and support, developing means for expressing their creative and energetic talents in fulfilling and useful (including profitable) ways, and striving for balanced lives of fun, relaxation and work. Busters are just beginning to enter their child-bearing years, so the effect of children on Buster church connections will be interesting to watch. However, the church would be unwise to assume that Buster parents will respond positively to large, slick programs in the way that Boomers did. Busters seem to be more interested in providing communities for themselves and, thus, for their children. Busters are likely to have the goal of raising confident, happy children who know how to laugh and play freely with children, not only in their own neighborhoods, but all over the world as well. The Internet and foreign travel make the world much more of a global community than it has ever been before. Churches that offer opportunities for such community-building and relationship interaction are more likely to attract Buster parents than churches that offer the most intense programs and organized outings for children. This is seen most dramatically in churches that have a strong small-group ministry. Unlike the "program churches" that have been so essential in serving the families of Baby Boomers, "relationship churches" are likely to become prime communities of faith for Busters and their families. For example, one of the United Methodist campus ministries on the West Coast has given up its long history of monthly speakers and political rallies. Instead, the chaplain hosts a weekly dinner and discussion time in his home, where the students set the agenda and determine the subjects of discussion each week. At a time when many mainline campus ministries are fading, this ministry is exploding with new students each week.

In the Buster generation, theological questions range from "Who is God" to "Who am I?" Busters are asking things like "Where do I fit into this world? What is my purpose? How do I develop meaningful relationships? Whom can I trust? Do people actually care about each other? How do I help my children to care about others? Does God make any difference at all?" These questions can be troubling to mature Christians who have never answered some of these questions in their own lives. They can be frustrating to other Followers who think that the answers should be obvious. Nevertheless, questions like these are worth addressing in the church. Not only do they help Followers and Seekers alike to travel their spiritual journeys to new levels, but also these questions help churches to talk about relationships and personhood in new and meaningful ways.

Which brings us to the final generation of Americans at the close of this 20th century: the millennial generation of Birthers. The Birthers are being born into smaller families than Baby Boomers knew, and are being inundated with attention and material possessions. The Seekers of this generation are likely to first hear about the church from their friends since so few of them will be raised in families that attend church regularly. The Seekers of this generation are likely to be very interested in relevant church traditions that help to stabilize and strengthen society. Also, the Seekers of this generation will need the support of a God who is big enough and a theology that is broad enough to handle the vast changes that our society will face over the next 50 years.

Both of the younger generations are fast-paced and highly stimulated. Attention spans are not as short as you would think, if the stimulus is strong enough. Many Busters and Birthers will spend hours on-line playing one video game or in one chat room of conversation. On the other hand, lack of stimulus will shorten attention spans to as little as 1 to 2 minutes. When Busters and Birthers channel surf, they are as likely to watch a series of 30-second commercials that fascinate them as they are to watch an 8-minute sitcom segment that seems repetitive or predictable. When Busters and Birthers do homework for teachers or projects for employers, they will probably do so sitting at the coffee table with a television show, a compact disc, and even a computer all whizzing around at the same time. It is yet to be seen how loyal Birthers will be in their likes and dislikes, but Busters will continue to change with the wind. What is popular this year will be passé next year; what excites this month may very well seem droll and boring next month. These are not generations who are interested in attending churches that follow a trend one year later. But these are generations who will respond to opportunities for community and connection. Busters and Birthers will face more change than any generation in American history. If the church can become a place of flexible stability where change is a part of life, but does not control life, Busters and Birthers will accept and even embrace the church's place in their lives. If, however, the church continues as a harbinger of tradition for tradition's sake and a rejecter of change for fear of controversy, Busters and Birthers are not likely to even enter the doors, let alone stick around for a life time of spiritual journeying.

The Church

For each of the generations of Seekers, the church is not offering much in the way of welcome or relevance. Even when a Seeker enters the church, churchgoers expect Seekers to look and act like Followers. Dress codes, although not stated, certainly exist. Such dress codes are even more confusing in a day and age where some churches are informal and others are formal. The Seeker will not know which "dress code" applies until they have entered the worship setting, sometimes overdressed and often underdressed. In either case, Seekers risk those strange stares and awkward feelings of inadequacy in churches where all of the Followers dress similarly.

Most worship leaders expect seekers to know what Followers know. Worship service language, newsletter acronyms, bulletins and worship order abbreviations and symbols all point to an assumption that people have worshipped with this community previously. Most Protestants have experienced the confusion of not knowing when to sit or stand or what to say while attending a Catholic service. Similar confusion is typical of Seekers' experience, no matter what the denominational choice may be.

Too often, church leaders expect Seekers to believe what Followers believe. Sermons seem to assume that everyone present has accepted Christ into their lives. Stewardship drives and even many morning offerings are full of implications that everyone present has made a formal commitment to the church at some point. Questions, struggles, and doubts are seldom expressed openly in worship services. Often, these same questions, struggles, and doubts go unspoken and unheard in classes and small groups. Thus, the questions of Seekers in every generation, as noted above, are helpful to churches that wish to grow spiritually and relationally. Until these questions are addressed honestly and freely in the church, Seekers are not likely to turn to churches as places for pursuing a spiritual quest.

By contrast, in churches that welcome the uncertainties of Seekers, Followers are freer to acknowledge their shortcomings and admit that they often forget to seek God themselves. Churches that welcome Seekers create Followers who are better able to actually follow Christ. Perhaps the greatest gift that Seekers bring to a church is that constant reminder that the reason for coming to church is indeed to seek (and find) God. (Matthew 7:7–8 and Jeremiah 29:12–14)

As Followers begin to recognize the gifts that Seekers bring to the church, Followers will find it easier to answer God's call to reach out to Seekers. However, reaching Seekers is not as easy as it may sound. The needs and interests of Seekers may surprise many Followers. Worship services that have spoken so strongly to Followers for the last 25 years may seem like foreign experiences to Seekers who have been absent in worship for most of their lives. As churches begin to acknowledge God's call to reach Seekers, churches will need tools for reaching these Seekers. In subsequent chapters, we will explore some of those tools. As you read each chapter, think about the Seekers in your community. Imagine those same Seekers being ministered to with some of the tools we discuss. Then, adapt the tools in your mind to adjust to the specific needs of Seekers in your community. Together, Seekers and Followers of all generations can find ways of worshipping and growing on the Christian journey.

Notes

1. Researchers like Strauss and Howe in *Generations* (New York: Morrow, 1991) believe that in the new millennium, we will see this generation being birthed presently rebuilding much of the institutional stability that we have lost or destroyed in the late 20th century.

CHAPTER THREE

Creative Worship
For Tomorrow

New to the Pacific Northwest, I have visited a number of churches in the area. On a recent visit, I drove into a large church parking lot, followed the clearly marked directional signs, and entered a beautiful sanctuary. The deep red carpet was reminiscent of my childhood church, the octagonal design spacious and inviting, and the natural wood chancel furniture fitting for its harbor-town setting. But when I saw the comfortable, padded chairs arranged in small circles, I thought, "What kind of a service is this?!" An usher kindly explained that I was to follow the symbol on my bulletin to the same symbol on one of the circles of chairs. I wandered around the sanctuary, somewhat lost, seeking the star that matched my bulletin cover. After much hunting, I finally saw the small piece of paper indicating where "my" circle was located. I sat down and smiled shyly at the church members sitting around me (all wearing their large, shiny, new name tags). Despite my obvious discomfort at being a guest, I quickly realized that no one was going to say "hello" to me, perhaps because they too were surprised and inhibited by this circular arrangement. As a pastor, I empathized with the discomfort of this congregation. As a visitor, I resented their refusal to welcome me. The service began with lengthy announcements, and my mind wandered for several minutes while people popped up to tell of their favorite upcoming events. I wanted to enjoy the lovely chancel furniture, but my seat was facing the side wall of the sanctuary. All I could see were more chairs, one very plain stained glass window, and a host of musical instruments on the opposite side of the room. Finally, the announcements ended, we sang a hymn or two, we recited a prayer, and we listened to an explanation of why we were in circles. Apparently, I had visited on a day when the Strategic Planning Task Force was seeking congregational input on the long-term vision for the church. Ugh! How could I share my vision for a church I was attending for the first time?! However, as the process unraveled, I realized that they were hoping to prioritize evangelism, and I thought that I, as both pastor and visitor, could offer some valuable input. Funny, no one ever asked! The leader of our small circle monopolized our discussion time, selling her vision for the church. During this 40-minute visioning session, no opportunity for others to offer input was given. When the discussion came to a close, we continued to worship with more hymns and prayers. Ninety minutes after my arrival, all I wanted to do was leave and never come back. Then, the old man sitting next to me pounced. The same man who had not even peeped a "Hello" or gestured a welcoming smile when I sat next to him suddenly wanted my voice. Did I mention that I sing well? It can be a curse for a visitor; he wanted me to join their dreadful choir of 6, meet their choir director, and shake hands with their pastor. I was mortified. I wanted the floor to open up and swallow me whole, and I certainly did *not* want to visit this church again!

You should know that I am an ordained pastor of many years, a lifelong churchgoer, and an off-the-scale extrovert by any psychological or sociological standard. Yet, by the time I walked to my car, I felt exhausted, overwhelmed, ignored, but most of all used. I returned home to tell my husband that if I had been attending church for the first time, I would *never* want to enter a church service again. The experience was that distasteful. For many Seekers, my feelings of disorientation and being an outsider are the same reactions they experience while attending their first traditional or praise worship service.

Contrast my experience as visitor to that of Michelle, a teenage Seeker (of the Buster generation) who attended church for the first time in her life at the invitation of her friend Heidi. Heidi, the retired pastor's granddaughter and an active teenager in her church, regularly brought new friends to church and never hesitated to bring them to any and all church events. In Heidi's church, teenagers were not invited to attend worship and proceeded to Sunday School classes upon their arrival. This was "fall kickoff" day, so the teacher Mrs. Olesen was trying to grasp how much the students remembered from previous years of Sunday School. She invited each student to name one book of the Bible. Seeker Michelle wished on every star that she had ever seen that the circle would begin in her direction first. Michelle could name "Genesis," which she remembered from the newest *Star Trek* movie as the name of some biblical writing. She froze with fear when the circle proceeded in the other direction, leaving Michelle to be the 15th person to name a book. Next to Michelle, a long-time member of that Sunday School class was sweating it out in his own way by quietly opening his Bible to the table of contents and glancing down for some book that had not yet been named. Michelle gazed over his shoulder and had her answer. When Mrs. Olesen called on her, Michelle quietly said "job" (pronounced like a means of employment). Amidst the snickers of her classmates, Mrs. Olesen said "That's correct, Michelle, job or Job as some pronounce it is a book in the Bible. Next person." The other students immediately quieted their snickers, and Michelle suddenly felt like she belonged. In that moment, Mrs. Olesen had used her excellent teaching instincts to overcome any prejudice her own biblical knowledge might have aroused. She had helped the Seeker to feel like one of the Followers.

When we plan worship for the Seeker, we need to understand the Seeker's experience of our faith community, the Seeker's need for spiritual nourishment, and the Seeker's response to our attempt at welcoming visitors into an already-existing faith community. In developing this understanding, we develop "seeker-sensitive" eyes. Developing such eyes is not an easy task, but an exciting and challenging one for the Follower who yearns to relate to Seekers. As Dennis Gill, music director for King of Glory Lutheran Church in Dallas says, "It is indeed a strange land to navigate through [when seeking to understand Seekers]."[1]

An important element of any Seeker service is a well-trained team of ushers, greeters, and worship leaders who understand a Seeker's needs. Seekers feel more at ease when ushers explain where to go if visitors need a bathroom or what to do if visitors do not understand the bulletin or program. Seekers are welcomed as "insiders" when greeters help visitors find their way to the nursery or Sunday School and then back to the worship space. Seekers appreciate ushers and greeters who escort them to a seat with plenty of space. Seekers find their bearings in this strange new world called "church" when they encounter ushers who explain how the bulletin or program, hymnal, and Bible function during the service. Seekers appreciate the warm environment created by worship leaders who never lapse into "insider/outsider" language when making announcements or preaching sermons. The experience of a Seeker is much like that of an English-speaking US citizen who is lost in a foreign country. For the Seeker, this world of Christian worship can also be a strange land through which to navigate. Finding a person who can and will give directions in English is like finding an angel of mercy. Even traditional worship services can provide such angels with properly trained worship leaders.

Most traditional worship and praise services assume a great familiarity with the Christian tradition. When we Followers make such assumptions, our language and our attitude are usually welcoming only to "insiders" who know our language and our tradition. We may say things such as "Join us for coffee hour in the fellowship hall," or "Visitors are invited to the chancel for a tour following today's service." Fellowship halls and chancels are not common terms to the secular ear. When we use this "insider" language, we send a message that those who do not understand are not "us"; they are "outsiders." Inclusive language takes on a whole new meaning in this context. For Seekers, the primary language issue is not whether we refer to God as "He" or "Mother." For Seekers, the primary issue is whether we image a God who welcomes all persons into a holy worship space. Seekers are outsiders to the church in so many other ways that language should not be another reason for them to feel excluded.[2]

Since Seekers come from such a broad variety of backgrounds, one style of "seeker-oriented" worship will seldom fit the niche of every community. In contrast to other worship and evangelism resources that suggest Seekers be separated from Followers in worship settings, I believer that Seekers can and should be welcome to worship with Followers. Any style of Seeker worship can be worship appropriate for Followers of any maturity level. In the Book of Acts, there are no indications that separate worship events were offered to differentiate new Christians, or non-Christians, from longer-term Christians (remembering, of course, that none of the Christians in the Book of Acts would meet most of our modern-day criteria for long-term Christians). When Paul or Peter preached, he preached to any and all who would listen. When the community gathered, any and all who wished to share food and fellowship were welcomed. When the community worshipped, all who wished were invited to experience God's presence in the midst of that early Christian community.

Unfortunately, the late 20th century has brought a new approach to Christian community. In too many cases, churchgoers expect all Christian worship, education, fellowship, and communal eating needs to be fulfilled in a 90-minute segment each week. In so doing, we expect the preacher's message time to answer every faith question and practical living issue that has arisen in our lives this past week. Too many worshippers look to 3 hymn selections or 30 minutes of praise music to fulfill our every need to worship God with praise and song for the next 7 days. The pastoral or community prayer time is somehow expected to answer every prayer request that has built in our hearts in the previous week and to address the needs that our sister and brother Christians have for us to pray on their behalves. And, of course, we also want to make public announcements during that 90-minute weekly segment about any upcoming events that are near and dear to our hearts. Unfortunately, the communal worship of God on a weekly basis was never meant to encompass such a vast array of needs, nor is it capable of doing so.

On the other hand, some contemporary theologians have decided that this worship experience is so crucial to the Christian walk that it is only to be available to Followers on that walk. The presence of Seekers might somehow demean the experience, invalidate God's presence in the community, or "water down" the worship service such that mature Christians would not experience all that they desire in this holy time. In every argument advocating the separation of Seekers from Followers, one motivation seems to ring loud and clear: fear, Fear, FEAR! Different fears arise for different folks, but I suspect that two fears guide these arguments. First, our own selfish needs as Followers might not be met if we had to welcome Seekers. The Gospel message is clear that such selfish fears can lead to legalism and hollow worship, the opposite of what Jesus called for when he requires Followers to worship in spirit and truth (John 4:23–24). In Romans 7:6, Paul reminds Followers that investing ourselves in the letter of the law leads to death when Christ wants to offer us life. The second fear is more self-giving and yet equally damaging in terms of living out the Gospel. I sense that many church leaders opt for the separate "Seeker event" out of fear that they may be incapable of welcoming the outsider into an "insider" experience of worship. Jesus' message in the Gospels is equally clear that God's priority will always go to the "outsider" not to the "insider" (Matthew 9:10–13; Luke 15), and the realization that we may have drifted to the side of those "insider" Pharisees is somewhat disconcerting. As another student, Betty Strawn of Asbury UMC in Albuquerque, said in one of my classes: "We have a responsibility to train all members of a congregation in the 'art' of presenting a welcoming spirit to visitors."[3] When Followers remember that responsibility and receive proper training, congregations are better able to overcome fears of inadequately responding to Seekers.

In spite of Followers' fears, people's spiritual needs will be met. God will see to that. If Followers do not find ways to welcome Seekers into Christ's midst, Seekers will find other ways to approach the throne of grace. God will see to it that some form of the Body of Christ will be addressing the spiritual needs of Seekers and Followers. The question remains as to whether currently-existing churches are prepared to be that Body of Christ for the 21st century. At the end of the 20th century, worship services tend to fall into one of three categories: Traditional, Praise, or Seeker services. Although many persons who have experienced only one of these worship styles are afraid that other styles would be too different to every feel comfortable, the three styles do have some things in common.

Styles of Worship for the Twenty-First Century

TRADITIONAL WORSHIP

refers to liturgical services, often lectionary based, which focus on word, song, and sacrament in the historical traditions of the Church.

PRAISE SERVICES

refers to those worship experiences which focus on praise songs, scripture, extemporaneous speaking, and traditional words of praise. Written words are seldom used.

SEEKER SERVICES

refers to those worship experiences designed for persons who have not attended "traditional worship" or have rejected the institutional church. Focus is on journeying together, using secular media rather than traditional service elements.

Seeker-Sensitive Potential in Various Worship Styles

TRADITIONAL WORSHIP	PRAISE SERVICES	SEEKER SERVICES
Insider/Outsider	Insider/Outsider	Visitor-Friendly
or	*or*	*and*
Visitor-Friendly	Visitor-Friendly	Seeker-Friendly
and/or	*and/or*	
Seeker-Friendly	Seeker-Friendly	

INSIDER/OUTSIDER = experiences which require knowledge of the pattern of worship, the materials used, the words spoken and actions performed, and/or the location of events surrounding worship

VISITOR-FRIENDLY = experiences designed so that participants need not have any prior experience with this particular community, denomination, or worship style.

SEEKER-FRIENDLY = experiences designed for persons with no prior experience of attending worship. Avoids use of traditional elements such as sanctuary, hymnals, bulletins, traditional creeds, or memorized liturgy. May utilize secular media.

Comparing Worship Styles

Traditional	Praise	Seeker
Begins meditatively, sometimes socially	Begins with high energy and participation	Begins with high energy May/may not be participatory
Service flow is predictable; Order of worship follows liturgical format: praise —word —response	Service flow is often same; Order of worship is praise-oriented: series of praise songs & prayer, biblical message	Flow of the service may vary; Order journey-oriented around a common theme, often with much music and/or drama
Use of traditional liturgy	Traditional liturgy used sparsely	No use of memorized traditional liturgy
Strong scriptural base (often lections)	Topic or lection-based; sometimes biblical series	Thematic or topical base
More formal (robes/vestments)	Less formal; fewer vestments	Informal (no robes; perhaps jeans & T-shirts)
Service led by pastor & liturgist (may be team-planned)	Service led by worship team (May be team-planned)	Led and planned by worship team
Printed bulletin or memorized liturgy is essential	No printed bulletin or program	Printed program in outline format
Service may be followed by church school, fellowship hour with juice, coffee, & pastries	Service may be followed by church school, fellowship hour with juice, coffee, & pastries	Service may be followed by snacks, light meal, or full meal with fellowship activities

Traditional	Praise	Seeker
Sermon may be scriptural or topical	Sermon is scriptural, and often practical	Sermon is practical and non-judgmental
Sermon is often proclamation: "Let me tell you"	Sermon is often pedagogical, sometimes judgmental: "Let me teach you"	Sermon is invitational "What do you think? What do you wonder about?"
Sermon from pulpit: "I have knowledge to share."	Sermon is often from center, floor "We're learning together"	Sermon is from center, floor, often seated "Join me on the journey"
Media usually limited to organ, piano, choir, printed bulletins, spoken word (Youth participation may occasionally vary these limits)	Multimedia (less use of organ, more use of piano and electronic instruments) Use of drama & other arts occasionally	Multimedia Use of drama very effective May utilize various arts (visual, dance, video, etc.) The more variety the better
Music led by choir & organ	Music led by singers & instruments (guitar, piano, etc) May use accompaniment tapes	Music provided by pop, jazz, or country band (may use pre-recorded music if video is included)
Music based on hymnody, fluctuating between upbeat & slower, meditative	Music very lively & upbeat, often throughout service; slow songs used around prayer	Music of very high quality, often very lively, sometimes meditative for specific purpose
Familiar hymns primary; choir leads for classical & contemporary hymnody	Familiar praise choruses are central musical component	Familiar pop songs are often the central musical component

Despite some similarities between all worship styles, current Traditional and Praise services would need to integrate a number of Seeker elements in order to effectively minister with Seekers in a worship setting. However, only very courageous and unique congregations are taking the necessary steps to blend in such Seeker-friendly elements.

Thus, as we approach the 21st century, we will see an increasing number of worshipping communities springing up in towns and cities across the country. Many of these communities will explore alternative styles and methods of worship. As mentioned above, the question remains whether or not those communities will be related to currently existing churches. Seekers who are attracted to such alternatives in Christian worship may fall into one of several categories: **Unchurched Seekers, Anti-Church Seekers, Sunday Schooled Seekers,** and **Converted Seekers.** Although other categories of Seekers may arise in the coming years, most Seekers today fall into one or some combination of these four categories. Most Seekers who visit churches will have some aspects of more than one of these categories. Nevertheless, the categories can be helpful delineation points in the Follower's search to understand Seekers more clearly.

As you design your worship services to be "seeker-sensitive," you may choose to focus on one particular type of Seeker or simply keep in mind the various factors and aim for "Seekers" in general. In the more generalized case, you will want to merge the various suggestions offered here into the particular hybrid that will most effectively reach your community of Seekers into the midst of Followers. If you are, however, designing a specific Seeker ministry, it will be most effective if you concentrate on the type of Seeker you believe God is calling you to minister with. At the very least, every church who takes seriously God's call to make disciples of all the nations (Matthew 28:19) needs to be striving to make Followers of every Seeker brought into the church's midst. In order to do so, the prime entry point into the Christian community—worship—needs to be designed in ways that welcome the Seekers onto the Christian journey. Such a welcoming experience helps Seekers to see that following Christ leads to a spiritual place of unconditional love and wholeness in the presence of God.

BASICS FOR WELCOMING SEEKERS

- Understandable worship language and message themes
- Integration of secular resources and language into the sacred experience
- Written and verbal instructions that explain everything expected of the worshiper (when to sit, when to stand, when to sing, when to speak)
- Multiple means of communicating (verbal and visual—written in handouts or songbooks, written on overhead or video projections, and displayed in artwork and physical gestures)
- Friendly greeters and ushers who can and do offer guidance and instruction about all aspects of the worship service and church offerings
- Worship and music leadership that is warm and welcoming
- Sacraments that are offered to, but not required of, all participants
- Comfortable seating areas, with easy access for those who wish to leave during the worship service
- Clear directional signs to rest rooms, nursery areas, parking, worship space, and reception area
- Tasty food and a friendly reception time prior to and/or following the worship experience

The Unchurched Seeker
Seeking in a Foreign Land

"If you're looking for perfect people, you won't find them here."

Unchurched Seekers are persons who have not been exposed to a Christian worshiping community. Some grew up in homes with parents who found neither the time nor the interest to affiliate with a church community even while confessing a belief in God. Some grew up in homes of other faiths or homes opposed to organized religion. Most often, however, the Unchurched Seeker comes from a family that, quite frankly, has not given organized religion or God much thought. Yet, many adult children from such homes yearn for a spiritual community and, when welcomed, will turn to a church to fulfill their spiritual needs. Unchurched Seekers may hesitate coming to worship, not so much out of opposition to organized religion as from the fear that they will be judged for past lifestyles or absence from church. Unchurched Seekers need to hear, "Christians aren't perfect, just forgiven." Indeed, the slogan, "If you're looking for perfect people, you won't find them here" is an effective invitation to the Unchurched Seeker service.

Worship leaders cannot assume that Unchurched Seekers are familiar with any element of traditional worship. Services for the Unchurched Seekers cannot assume *anything*! In other words, Unchurched Seekers are not the types of church visitors who will necessarily understand when to sit or stand, what "churchy" words or instructions mean, or even how to dress appropriately for the worship service. Worship planners will need to utilize the best "seeker-sensitive eyes" available to design worship that does not assume a knowledge and understanding of the patterns and parts of worship. Worship that welcomes the Unchurched Seeker may incorporate traditional elements of worship, but these elements will need to be explained and defined when used.

Worship for the Unchurched Seeker need not include traditional worship elements if such elements are not crucial to your church's understanding of faith maturity. However, including traditional elements will help the Unchurched Seeker to feel welcome when visiting other faith communities that are

TRADITIONAL ELEMENTS OF WORSHIP
often include

- Memorized prayers such as "The Lord's Prayer" ("Our Father")
- Memorized hymns or songs such as "Praise God from Whom All Blessings Flow" or "Lord, Be Glorified"
- Memorized creeds or readings
- Headings unique to church publishing such as "Offertory" or "Altar Call"
- Language unique to church or worship settings such as "pulpit," "tithes," "bulletin," or "registration pad"
- Forms such as Prayers of the People with a memorized response or responsive Psalter singing
- Written liturgical forms that assume an understanding of their use (bold print indicates people recite the line)
- Unexplained written symbols (asterisks used to indicate standing)
- Unexplained visual symbols, such as a cross or a dove
- Worship space with pulpit, altar, lectern, and pews
- Musical styles unique to the church (hymns or praise choruses)
- Leadership styles unique to the church (formal choirs, acolytes, worship leaders in liturgical vestments)
- Reading of 4 lections each week, usually without explanation of all the readings and their relevance to modern life
- Sacraments are offered or served

not attentive to the needs of Unchurched Seekers. The Unchurched Seeker has entered a foreign land by attending your worship service; helping them to learn the "native language" of church tradition will help them in your worship setting and in other worship services these Seekers may one day visit. Inclusion and explanation of several traditional elements at every worship gathering, however, may become a bit cumbersome. To avoid being pedantic, the "teaching ministry" of such worship services can be offered in moderation. Although the worship service for the Unchurched Seeker may appear too non-traditional, worship teams might want to remember that present traditions were once also new. Traditions became so because they were at one time warm, inviting, and inclusive. The traditions developed in Unchurched Seeker services may become important traditions in the lives of both Seekers and long-term church members. Even if designing worship for the Unchurched Seeker seems constraining initially, over time a worship planning team will find the challenge exciting and joyous.

Ideally, worship for the Unchurched Seeker contains these crucial elements:

1. Upbeat, fast-paced mood or intentional meditation and reflection

2. Practical, down-to-earth messages

3. Use of secular terms for the parts of worship

4. Definitions or explanations of any traditional elements of worship

5. Use of secular resources alongside scriptural or traditional resources

6. Use of modern, understandable language, such as that used in *USA Today*, *People*, or FOX Television.

7. Leadership that is warm and welcoming

8. Leadership that explains or role models each event in worship

9. Leadership that does not assume prior knowledge of the space, the resources, or the purpose for gathering

10. Leadership that welcomes, but does not require, participation

11. Musical leadership that is energetic and inviting

12. Musical leadership that welcomes, but does not require, participation

13. A creatively designed service that does not depend too heavily on either verbal or written instructions

14. A creatively designed service that incorporates several of the senses

15. A creatively designed service that is stimulating visually, musically, physically, mentally, and emotionally

Two examples of appropriate worship services for the Unchurched Seeker (*Worship Figure A and Figure B*) may be helpful as your team plans its first few services. As you review the services, note the use of explanatory notes, common language, secular resources, and creative worship resources.

Figure A offers a meditative style of worship for the Unchurched Seeker who needs an opportunity to slow down and relax during worship. The centering time uses a Native American prayer form facing the four directions to prepare for a time of worship. An example of a Christian version of such preparation time can be found in *The United Methodist Book of Worship*, #470. The centering song (#197) can be accompanied by a drum and is repeated in chant format to help persons clear their minds and connect with the Holy. The reading from Matthew's Gospel could be delivered dramatically or read by a good storyteller. The Thoughts (or sermon) are practical and down-to-earth, offering a connection between the scripture and daily life. All written resources can be projected on an overhead screen for those who do not want to shuffle pieces of paper or find page numbers in a book.

Worship for the Unchurched Seeker
Worship Figure A
Welcome!
This morning, we will focus on caring for one another as sacred beings, seeking to unify the differences that may separate us.

MUSIC FOR MEDITATION & FELLOWSHIP John Michael Talbot
"Nocturne/One Dark Night"

OPENING THOUGHTS

A TIME FOR CENTERING "Christ, Our Center"

SONG OF CENTERING "Shawnee Traveling Song"

PRAYER SONG "Jesus, Remember Me" Hymnal, p. 488

A TIME FOR PRAYER AND SUPPORT

VIDEO "Everybody Hurts" Performed by R.E.M.

READING Matthew 6:25–33

THOUGHTS ON LIVING THE LESSON

SONG OF HOPE *"Seek Ye First" Hymnal, p. 405

CLOSING WORDS

4

❖   ❖   ❖

- Ushers are available at all times to answer your questions or direct you to rest rooms, child-care rooms, or other places in our church.
- Hymnals (songbooks) and Bibles are available in the shelves in front of your seats.
- Children's handouts & coloring packets are available from ushers at all entrances.
- Children may worship with you or attend Children's Activity Hour in the Education wing, north of the sanctuary.
- Please join us for refreshments downstairs following the service today. Coffee, tea, juice, fruit, and doughnuts will be served.

Thanks for joining us at First Community Church, 111 Main Street, Anywhere, USA! If we can assist you further, please call us at 555–1111.

Traditional Worship for the Unchurched Seeker
Worship Figure B

WELCOME!
We welcome all who enter our doors each day!
Everyone's participation is invited.
Freedom to observe is also welcomed.

- **Bolded words** indicate you may join in the speaking.
- ✦indicates that those who are able are invited to stand.

❖　　❖　　❖

GATHERING MUSIC

GATHERING WORDS & MUSIC   Written & Performed by Amy Grant

"Love Has a Hold on Me"

✦PRAYER

Give us, Señor, a little sun, a little happiness, and some work.
Give us a heart to comfort those in pain.
Give us the ability to be good, strong, wise, and free,
    so that we may be generous with others and with ourselves.
Finally, Señor, let us all live as your own one family. Amen.

✦SONG "Cuando El Pobre" ("When the Poor Ones")   Hymnal, p. 434
    (Feel free to sing in the language of your choice.)

SCRIPTURE READING   Micah 6:6–8   Bible, p. XX

A MESSAGE FOR TODAY

SONG   "Helping Hand"   Amy Grant

PRAYERS OF THE PEOPLE

LORD'S PRAYER   (printed on overhead transparency)   Hymnal p. 895

✦SONG   "Lord, You Give the Great Commission" Hymnal p. 584

✦PARTING WORDS and MUSIC FOR DEPARTURE

Figure B represents a blended Unchurched Seeker service (a service incorporating traditional elements in a way that is inclusive of Seekers). Even in a traditional service of this sort, written resources are projected on an overhead screen and the service avoids the use of "churchy" language. When reciting the Lord's Prayer, the worship planning team teaches this traditional prayer to the Seekers by displaying the text on the overhead screen. Worship leaders might also explain why it is called the Lord's Prayer and note that there are several different versions spoken in Christian churches. Popular recorded music is interspersed with hymns and church songs, helping persons to merge familiar resources from their everyday lives with the traditional tools of Christian worship. When using taped music or even live music, creative worship planners may wish to also utilize slide shows or dance to further illustrate the themes of the music and lyrics. Addressing more senses than just the ears can be a very helpful way of reaching Seekers and Followers more consistently, particularly those whose attention spans may be distracted easily.

If stereotypes about the use of overhead projectors or videos in worship are troubling your worship planning team, you may want to help the planners connect worship with our contemporary world. Worship styles have long been a reflection of, or at least in relationship with, the situations in which worship leaders and participants find themselves living. In early American days, that meant worship in log cabins or under canopy tents for earthy revivals. In 1950s America, that often meant worship in large and beautifully-decorated spaces with well-crafted formal structures. Today, many persons today are oriented toward the screen. We program our VCRs on the TV screen, we catch the stock report on the Internet screen, we play games on our computer screen, and we enjoy most of our entertainment on the TV or movie screen. As the number of persons who read news and information from papers and magazines continues to dwindle, this trend is likely to continue. The Seeker service can reflect this current trend by moving away from the printed word and toward projected words and images. In this way, the Seeker service relates more clearly to the real situation that most Seekers and Followers find themselves living with on a daily basis.

Sacraments can be a part of the Unchurched Seeker service when they are open to all who attend the service and desire to participate. If sacraments are performed in a Seeker service, the basic meaning of the sacrament may be explained during the service—but with care, for sacraments by their very nature are experiences of mystery not logic and science.

Bulletins or programs are an option for any Seeker Service, although any worshiper should be able to worship without one in hand. Thus, written instructions can also be verbalized. For the many people who like to have something to take away with them, a program can help them remember their experience of your church. Printing announcements, church address and phone number, pastor's name and number or address are all helpful ways of connecting with the Unchurched Seeker. If using printed resources (in hand or on screen), use of white space is essential. People need to be able to scan quickly without the hindrance of wordiness or crowded pages.

The Anti-Church Seeker
Seeking in a Forbidden Land

> "If you're looking for stained glass windows or an organ, you won't find them here."

The Anti-Church Seeker is often someone who has known the Church intimately and become disillusioned. The Anti-Church Seeker would also refer to someone who harbors a negative stereotype about organized religion without any particular experience of the Church. The divisive work of the Moral Majority and the public downfall of many televangelists like Jimmy Swaggart and Jim Bakker in the 1980's spawned and nurtured much of today's Anti-Church sentiment. Anti-Church Seekers are perhaps the smallest segment of Seekers in our society today. These Seekers are also the least likely to ever walk into a church building. Yet, their passion against organized religion is often the shadow side of a deep yearning for a faith community. Anti-Church Seekers, thus, need a faith community that does not prompt reminders of the land of hypocrisy, condemnation, or pain that they have forbidden themselves to visit.

The Anti-Church Seeker may be of any age or background. Many Unchurched and Sunday Schooled Seekers may even harbor certain Anti-Church attitudes that worship planners will want to be aware of. Stereotypes of the Anti-Church Seeker are as prevalent and inaccurate as these Seekers' stereotyping of the Church. It is safest to assume nothing about this group except that they will very likely test and judge the leaders and participants of any worship experience or religious event with a critical eye. Ministering with Anti-Church Seekers most often begins with an open mind and a ready ear to hear about the needs and concerns of these Seekers. With good listening, Followers seek to understand who these Seekers are and where God is leading Anti-Church Seekers as they enter the Christian community. Reaching Anti-Church Seekers is far from easy, and it troubles me that so many of the books written on Seekers assume that all Seekers fall into this category. Although reaching the Anti-Church Seeker is likely to be more difficult than reaching Unchurched or Sunday Schooled Seekers, ministry with Anti-Church Seekers can be very fulfilling. Churches considering this type of ministry will want to carefully consider God's calling for their mission and ministry. If searching for the Anti-Church Seeker is in your church's mission and vision, additional training in pastoral care and sensitivity awareness may be necessary.

When planning worship for the Anti-Church Seeker, it is best to do so with an acceptance of the critical eye that will watch your leadership and your service of worship. Every element of the service will need to be of high quality and careful planning. However, the service should also feel "real," for any service that feels phony is likely to fuel the negative stereotypes that turned Anti-Church Seekers off in the first place. "Moderation in all things," as Aristotle would advise, is a good guideline when planning worship for the Anti-Church Seeker.

Since this Seeker often views the Church as a forbidden land for persons with integrity, a worship setting apart from the church building is best. Ideally, worship for the Anti-Church Seeker occurs in property not even owned by a church or religious institution. Church camps and affiliated universities may be appropriate settings if their church affiliation is not emphasized. When planning worship for the Anti-Church Seeker, it is best not to include any traditional elements of worship. Even for the Anti-Church Seeker who feels great familiarity with traditional worship, tradition is dangerous territory. Any given tradition may symbolize their reason for leaving the Church in the first place. For the Anti-Church Seeker who carries stereotypes without experience of the Church, traditional elements of worship may well prompt the same stereotypes—even when presented in a caring and welcoming manner.

However, because of this Seeker's "shadow side," she or he may welcome an opportunity to share in the spiritual journey of others—as long as that journey differs significantly from a journey toward traditional church membership. Thus, Anti-Church Seekers may walk into a community center or campground for secular events and find themselves curious about an advertisement for a worship experience in that same setting. One of the most compelling ads I have seen for a worshipping community states, "If you're looking for stained glass or an organ, you won't find it here." This invitation is likely to attract the Anti-Church Seeker as it honestly advertises that traditional trappings of Christian worship are not a part of this Christian community's worship and gatherings.

Worship for the Anti-Church Seeker is similar to that for the Unchurched Seeker (Elements 6–15), but differs significantly in its overt avoidance of any traditional elements. Ideally, the elements of Anti-Church Seeker Worship include:

1. Upbeat, fast-paced mood or intentional meditation and reflection

2. Practical, down-to-earth messages

3. Use of secular terms for the parts of worship

4a. Avoiding any use of traditional elements of worship (no altars, pulpits, traditional prayers, or traditional symbols such as the cross)

5a. Use of secular resources alongside scripture (avoids traditional liturgical forms)

6. Use of modern, understandable language, such as that used in *USA Today*, *People*, or FOX Television.

7. Leadership that is warm and welcoming

8. Leadership that explains or role models each event in worship

9. Leadership that does not assume prior knowledge of the space, the resources, or the purpose for gathering

10. Leadership that welcomes, but does not require, participation

11. Musical leadership that is energetic and inviting

12. Musical leadership that welcomes, but does not require, participation

13. A creatively designed service that does not depend too heavily on either verbal or written instructions

14. A creatively designed service that incorporates several of the senses

15. A creatively designed service that is stimulating visually, musically, physically, mentally, and emotionally

Elements 4 and 5 are unique to the Anti-Church Seeker worship service, and thus are noted with "a." These two decisions in worship design arouse great controversy among worship planners, so a bit of explanation may be helpful. Regarding Element 4, I trust that the church can maintain its long historic strength even if some worshipping communities do not re-en-act long-standing traditions. It can be helpful to explain and incorporate tradition into the lives of those Seekers who desire to worship in other faith communities. However, this is not likely to be the case for the Anti-Church Seeker. Anti-Church Seekers are not likely to trust any faith community apart from the one that they have grown to accept (namely yours if your Anti-Church Seeker ministry is successful). The Anti-Church Seeker may grow to great maturity in his or her faith walk with God and still refuse to accept the church's place in faith development. This Seeker is not a likely candidate for church shopping when relocated to another community. If the Anti-Church Seeker grows to a point where she or he wishes to know more about the traditions of the Church, such teaching is best handled in small group settings apart from worship. Again, any given tradition may evoke painful memories or vivid stereo-types. At a church interview, I amazed a homophobic church moderator when I introduced him to my handsome husband; the moderator assumed that all clergywomen were lesbians. Stereotypes abound, even amongst churchgoers! In one of my churches, I met a former Catholic woman who could never take communion at the altar rail because it reminded her of being molested on a home altar by her parents. Never underestimate the power of memory for the Anti-Church Seeker!

Regarding the use of scripture: God's Word, like God, is strong enough to withstand even the most vivid stereotypes and painful memories. A seminary colleague of mine told of one parishioner who came to her for counseling. The pastor dis-covered that the sacrifice of Jeptha's daughter (Judges 11:29–40) had been read repeatedly to this woman in child-hood. Her religious father used the scripture to defend his sexual and physical abuse of his young daughter. Rather than ignoring this painful part of scripture, the pastor utilized the same scripture to help the woman see Jeptha's (and the woman's father's) behavior as the inappropriate behavior and that of the daughter as innocence. The pastor then lifted the behavior of the biblical women who remembered Jeptha's daughter each year in their ritual on the mountain as a means for this woman to remember her pain, name the sins of her father, and reclaim her place in the sisterhood of women who worshipped God. If anything, the Seeker Service that denies scripture's place in worship only furthers stereotypes and buries memories. Using scripture carefully and gently in worship is an important element in re-claiming the scriptures as our own and overcoming the misuse and abuse that many people have experienced from Bible thumpers and proof-textors. When using scripture in worship, it should not be introduced by its liturgical title (the Gospel or Epistle or Old Testament), but it can be named if that is helpful as a teaching tool. ("Luke writes these words in his story of Jesus' life.") Scripture can seldom stand on its own in the Anti-Church Seeker service, so reading the four lections each week is risky business—particularly if any of the readings are controversial, confusing, or condemning. However, scripture can be read or dramatized and then explained through the message, through a question and answer period, or through a blending with other art forms or secular resources.

Examples of worship services for the Anti-Church Seeker (*Worship Figures C and D*) give some idea of how this might be done. As you review the services, note the use of common language and secular resources. Worship teams planning Anti-Church Seeker services may want to think of their congregation as foreigners visiting a land previously forbidden. Granted, the ban on such visits has probably been self-imposed by these Seekers; nevertheless, the mind set is there.

As with the Unchurched Seeker Service, programs (traditionally referred to as "bulletins") are an option, but any worshipper should be able to worship without one in hand. As Colleen Haley of First United Methodist Church in Columbus, Texas, said to me, "Bulletins strip the service of spontaneity and give the impression that worship is supposed to be done a 'certain way.'" For all Seekers, but particularly for the Anti-Church Seeker, the idea that there is a "right" or a "wrong" way to worship can be both intimidating and offensive. Thus, any necessary written instructions should be verbalized and kept to a minimum in this service since the Anti-Church Seeker may choose to observe rather than participate. A program/bulletin can help the Anti-Church Seeker remember the worship experience, but can also be designed in a flexible format so that worship leaders can add spontaneity to the worship experience. You will note in both *Figures C and D* that the programs simply name the different readings and songs that will be used during the service. The program does not list these elements in any particular order, allowing the worship leaders to respond flexibly to the Spirit's movement during the service. The flexible order also adds an element of surprise and anticipation to the service, particularly effective with younger Seekers.

An outline or note page (*Worship Figure C*) for helping the Seeker to hear the message can assist those inexperienced in listening to monologues or speeches. Some Seekers prefer open-ended note pages with the theme of the service or primary points of the message printed; others are helped by "fill-in" forms or questions. Printing invitations to non-threatening events (such as a dinner or recreation time) along with the worship leader's name and phone number can be helpful in connecting with the Anti-Church Seeker. In all print media, use of white space is essential. People need to be able to scan quickly without the hindrance of wordiness or crowded pages.

Alternative message styles are also particularly effective with the Anti-Church Seekers. Interactive message formats are helpful in reaching younger Seekers of any type, but the Anti-Church Seeker often comes with particular questions or concerns that need to be addressed promptly if the Anti-Church Seeker is ever to return to the worship service. Thus, I often utilize the Questioning Sermon (See Chapter 6) when offering a message in this style of worship service.

If weekly Holy Communion is a part of your church tradition, consider foregoing the tradition in the Anti-Church Seeker service. Holy Communion can be offered during a short chapel service before or after the Seeker service, if that is necessary for your church polity. Otherwise, sacraments are best introduced sparingly in the Anti-Church Seeker service. Although meaningful symbols for many Christians, the sacraments may be symbols of exclusion, anger, and pain for many Anti-Church Seekers. Consider introducing Holy Communion through the service of a Love Feast during a dinner celebration; consider introducing Baptism during a lakeside retreat. Be creative as you face this challenging issue in the life of a worship team planning services for the Anti-Church Seeker!

Worship for the Anti-Church Seeker Welcomes the Stranger!
Worship Figure C

MESSAGE

"THE LEGACY OF MARTIN LUTHER KING, JR."

SONGS AND VIDEOS

"Black and White"
Written & Performed by Michael Jackson

"I Believe"
Blessid Union of Souls

"Shed a Little Light"
Written & Performed by James Taylor

READINGS

Excerpt from **"I Have a Dream"**
by Dr. Martin Luther King, Jr.

A Reading from the Holy Bible
Matthew 5:1–12

❖   ❖   ❖

Worship Figure C (continued)

> Everyone's Invited!
> To What: A pizza party!
> When: After this evening's service
> Where: Across the hall

NOTES AS YOU LISTEN TO THE MESSAGE FOR TODAY

Matthew 5:1–12 January 25, 1996

"The Legacy of Martin Luther King"

Martin Luther King, Jr. Lived his life in pursuit of _____ for all people.

Dr. King was a _____, even when he called for resistance.

Jesus said, "Blessed are the peacemakers, for they will be called _____ __ ___."

Today, we live out the legacy of Dr. King when we strive for _____,

when we offer _____ to those who mourn,

when we offer _____ to those who are meek,

when we live _____ lives, becoming a light for the world,

when we are _____ even to those who can't accept mercy,

when we are ___ ___ ____, even when no one else notices,

when we are _____ in the midst of toil,

when we insist on _____ in the world around us,

even when we feel beat up and put down for living out this legacy. We all shed a little _____ when we join hands in unity with persons who differ from us.

We also have a _____!

The Seeker Service Welcomes the Stranger to Worship!

Worship Figure D

ORDER OF SERVICE
SEPTEMBER 27, 1997
4:00 p.m.

MESSAGE
"ME . . . WORRY?!"

For today's message, we will explore what it means to give up worrying that overwhelms us and what it means to begin to trust in God's love and goodness in our lives. As you read today's scripture passage (on the other side) you are invited to note any questions you have about this passage or theme on the 3x5 note cards provided. Ushers will collect them during the song "Everybody Hurts." As many questions as possible will be answered during our message today.

SONGS AND VIDEOS

"Seek Ye First"
Words & Music by Karen Lafferty

"What If God Was One of Us?"
Written & Performed by Joan Osborne

"Everybody Hurts"
Written & Performed by R.E.M.

READINGS

FROM THE HOLY BIBLE
Matthew 6:25–33

FROM "THE PROPHET" by Kahlil Gibran
"On Joy and Sorrow"

❖   ❖   ❖

Worship Figure D (continued)

A READING FROM THE HOLY BIBLE

Matthew 6:25–33

"Therefore I tell you, do not worry about your life, what you will eat or
what you will drink, or about your body, what you will wear.
   Is not life more than food, and the body more than clothing?

Look at the birds of the air; they neither sow nor reap nor gather into
barns, and yet your heavenly Father feeds them.
   Are you not of more value than they?

And can any of you by worrying add a single hour to your span of life?
   And why do you worry about clothing?
Consider the lilies of the field, how they grow;
      they neither toil nor spin,
yet I tell you, even Solomon in all his glory was not clothed like one of
these.

But if God so clothes the grass of the field, which is alive today and tomorrow is thrown into the oven,
   will he not much more clothe you—you of little faith?

Therefore do not worry, saying,
   'What will we eat?' or 'What will we drink?' or 'What will we wear?'
For it is the Gentiles who strive for all these things;
   and indeed your heavenly Father knows that you need all these things.

But strive first for the kingdom of God and his righteousness,
   and all these things will be given to you as well.[5]

The Sunday Schooled Seeker
Seeking in an Old Familiar Place

> **"If you think, 'I can't go home again,'
> welcome home!"**

   The Sunday Schooled Seeker has known and perhaps even
loved the Church as a Sunday School child. A Sunday Schooled
Seeker has sometimes been a "Sunday School drop-
off"—dropped off by parents who were not comfortable or

interested in attending church themselves. More often, a Sunday Schooled Seeker has been accompanied to church by parents who chose to worship without children. Parents, in search of a quiet moment for worship and solace away from the responsibilities of parenting, have chosen this option often since the 1970s. In either case, several generations of youth in our country have been, and are being, raised "in the church" without benefit of attending worship. Churches across this nation struggle with the debate between nurturing children's worship lives, and nourishing parents' spiritual and emotional needs; between educating our children in the faith, and including children in the worshipping community; between demanding two hours of busy families, and settling for the one hour that families are more willing to give. As the debate rages, the reality leaves many churched children with few if any worship experiences during their childhood years. These Sunday Schooled Seekers reach adulthood with little concept of the traditional elements of worship. These Seekers seldom know the memorized prayers, hymns, and creeds of traditional worship. Knowing when to sit or stand in worship or even how to use the tools of traditional worship such as hymnals or bulletins may be great mysteries for the Sunday Schooled Seekers. Yet, their spiritual yearning or desire to raise their own children in the church will most likely bring them back to church at some point as they seek God in an old, familiar place.

The Sunday Schooled Seeker was physically excluded from worship during childhood; in adulthood, this Seeker is emotionally excluded when the worship style assumes a prior knowledge of worship elements. Although the Sunday Schooled Seeker may have fond memories of Vacation Bible School leaders or church school teachers, their feelings toward other church leaders may be ambivalent. This Seeker may have resentments toward pastors who ignored them, parents who dropped them off, and a church that placed them in a box called the "Sunday School room"—where children were seldom seen or heard. Thus, the Sunday Schooled Seeker often leaves the church for many years after "graduation" from Sunday School. If the worship service welcomes only "insiders" immediately following such "graduation," a church can guarantee that the Sunday Schooled Seeker will not return anytime soon—if ever. Even the most traditional congregation is well advised to present a worship service that welcomes such Seekers.

When designing worship for the Sunday Schooled Seeker, assumptions are again dangerous territories. These Seekers may have heard many Bible stories in Sunday School, but may not have any idea how to find a scripture in the pew Bible. In worship, it is helpful to use a standardized pew Bible and include page numbers for reference if the congregation is expected to follow along as scripture is read or cited. Sunday Schooled Seekers may have heard the Doxology drifting down the stairs into the Christian education wing, but may never have sung it. Likewise, the Lord's Prayer may have been explained in a class, but reciting it weekly from memory is seldom done in Sunday School settings. Nevertheless, the Sunday Schooled Seeker is relatively familiar with the symbols of the faith and is often comfortable with the traditional means of expressing our faith through worship. As with the Unchurched Seeker, worship for the Sunday Schooled Seeker may incorporate traditional and symbolic elements, but should define and explain those elements as they are used. While teaching the traditions that are crucial to your community's faith journey, the Sunday Schooled Seeker service aims to strike a balance so that worship does not become an extended Sunday School lesson. Participation in the sacraments is particularly meaningful for this Seeker since such participation is highly symbolic of their inclusion in the total faith community—a community from which many such Seekers have felt excluded. A well-designed service for Sunday Schooled Seekers shows them that indeed, "You can go home again."

Worship for the Sunday-Schooled Seeker may be one of several different styles, but ideally contains these crucial elements:

1–3. Optional elements (see previous lists)

4. Definitions or explanations of any traditional elements of worship

5. Use of secular resources alongside scriptural or traditional resources

6s. Use of modern, understandable language, such as that used in *USA Today, People,* or FOX Television, even alongside more traditional scriptural images and theological language.

7. Leadership that is warm and welcoming

8. Leadership that explains or role models each event in worship

9. Leadership that does not assume prior knowledge of the space, the resources, or the purpose for gathering

10s. Leadership that gladly welcomes participation

11. Musical leadership that is energetic and inviting

12s. Musical leadership that gladly welcomes participation

13. A creatively designed service that does not depend too heavily on either verbal or written instructions

14. A creatively designed service that incorporates several of the senses (as good Sunday School lessons do)

15. A creatively designed service that is stimulating visually, musically, physically, mentally, and emotionally (as good Sunday school lessons are)

The Sunday Schooled Seeker service may include Elements 1–3, 4a, or 5a of the other styles of Seeker worship, but it need not. Sunday Schooled Seekers are very likely to enjoy participation (Elements 10s and 12s—unique to "Sunday Schooled Seekers") when the means for doing so is modeled and explained. Upbeat moods, secular language, practical, down-to-earth messages, and modern language (Elements 1–3 and 6) will enhance the worship services that speak best to these younger Seekers. However, many Sunday Schooled Seekers are prepared from their Sunday School training for the more traditional "churchy" mood that most worship services provide. Thus traditions do not necessarily have to be avoided, as they so often do for the Anti-Church Seeker (Elements 4a and 5a).

For the church that can hardly conceive of Seekers and their needs, the Sunday Schooled Seeker service is a good first step and a manageable goal. Blending Traditional or Praise (the 1980s version of traditional for many Sunday Schooled Seekers) with Seeker worship is a useful way to offer worship that welcomes and nourishes the Sunday Schooled Seeker. *Worship Figures E* and *F* show examples of how to design this style.

Traditional Worship Designed with the Sunday Schooled Seeker in Mind
Worship Figure E

Welcome to our service of worship today! Should you have a question during today's service, feel free to contact an usher at any time.
Ushers will offer directions and assist with any needs you might have.

- All who are able are invited to stand for song, prayer, or fellowship when standing is designated.
- All are invited to join in word or song when **bold** letters appear.
- Children are invited to remain in worship. All are welcome at our coloring corner, beside the main entrance.
- Prayer requests may be written on the pads in front of your seat. Ushers will collect them during the first song.

Worship Figure E (continued)

ORDER OF WORSHIP

Today's theme is "following God" as we celebrate the 3rd week of Epiphany, a season in the Christian year when we focus on Jesus as the light. During Epiphany, we study Jesus' early years as a traveling teacher, preacher, and healer.

GREETING (all who are able are invited to stand)
For it is the God who said, "Let light shine out of darkness," who has shown in our hearts
to give the light of the knowledge of the glory of God in the face of Jesus Christ.
Let us worship God together as we share in the light of Christ.*

OPENING SONG (standing) "Jesus Calls Us"   Hymnal, p. 398
Jesus calls us o'er the tumult of our life's wild, restless sea;
day by day his sweet voice soundeth,
saying "Christian, follow me!"

As of old the apostle heard it by the Galilean lake,
turned from home and toil and kindred,
leaving all for Jesus' sake.

OPENING PRAYER (standing)

**Almighty and everlasting God, you created us for yourself,
so that our hearts are restless until they find rest in you.
Grant to us hearts of love and strength that no selfish passion
or fear of weakness may hinder us from knowing and doing
your will.
In your light may we see life clearly, through Jesus Christ our
Lord.   Amen.***

SCRIPTURE READING   Isaiah 9:1–4   Bible, p. XX
(all may be seated; Bibles are available in the racks in front of you.)

A READING FROM PSALM 27
The Lord is my light and my salvation; whom shall I fear?
The Lord is the stronghold of my life; of whom shall I be afraid?
One thing I asked of the Lord, that will I seek after:
that I may dwell in the house of the Lord all the days of my life,
The Lord will hide me in shelter in the day of trouble;
I will sing and make melody to the Lord.

Worship Figure E (continued)

SCRIPTURE READING   Matthew 4:12–23   Bible, p. XX

SOLO   *"Lord, You Have Come to the Lakeshore"*   C. Gabarain
            (English words & Spanish translation may be found
                    on p. 344 of the hymnal)

MORNING MESSAGE
"Called, Loved, and Chosen"   Pastor Smith

PRAYER OF CONFESSION

**Everlasting God, you gave us the faith of Christ
    for a light to our feet amid the darkness of this world.
Have pity on us and others when, by doubting or denying your
light,
    we wander from your path of life.
Bring home the truth to our hearts and grant us to receive that
truth;
    through the same Jesus Christ our Lord. Amen.***

WORDS OF ASSURANCE

This is the message we have heard from God and proclaim to you,
that God is light and in God there is no darkness at all. If we walk in
the light, as God is in the light, we have fellowship with one another
and Christ cleanses us from all sin (1 John 1:5, 7).

SONG OF RESPONSE   Hymnal, p. 348
(all who are able are invited to stand)

Softly and tenderly Jesus is calling, calling for you and for me;
see on the portals he's waiting and watching,
watching for you and for me.
Come home (come home), come home (come home);
you who are weary, come home;
earnestly, tenderly, Jesus is calling, calling, O sinner, come home!

CLOSING WORDS (standing)

*For your order of worship, you would
include directions to after-church activities.*

As you review Worship Figure E, note the use of traditional
tools (such as the hymnal) without a requirement of knowing
how to use these tools. (Words are reprinted in the program;

this is an easy task for churches that are copyright licensed or seek permission from their denominational publisher for reprinting hymns.) Some traditional language is used ("prayer of confession"), but carefully. A good guideline to follow in the use of such language with the Sunday Schooled Seeker is to ask your Sunday School teachers if they use these words in their classes. "Confession," "assurance," "prayer," and "scripture" are all words found in many mainline Sunday School curriculums. "Sermon," "hymnal," and "chancel" are not as likely to be a part of the Sunday School vocabulary. When in doubt, avoid the "churchy" language!

Worship Figure F points to the easier style of blended worship, since praise services by their very nature were designed with the unchurched in mind. The danger, however, is the assumption that Praise services are still being designed with the unchurched in mind. Many church leaders think, "We offer a contemporary service. Everyone will feel welcome here." Visit another church's contemporary service and see how welcome you feel. They often sing different "favorite" praise choruses than the ones you know. The Praise service language usually assumes a knowledge of the particular building and worship space being used and almost always assumes an in-depth knowledge of faith terms and worship terms. "Come to the altar as you feel called," says the preacher. "What's an altar?" asks the Seeker. "Oh no! Is someone going to call on me?" exclaims the grown-up Sunday School student. As with blending the Traditional and Seeker services, when in doubt, avoid the "churchy" language! Making a video-tape of one of your own services can be a helpful first step in developing "Seeker-sensitive" eyes. A friend or colleague from a non-Christian background who is willing to help you to critique it with these ideas in mind can be very helpful in opening your mind to the needs of any Seeker.

The Praise Service That Doesn't Exclude

(Not a bulletin to be distributed,
but an order of worship for team to utilize)
Worship Figure F

Gathering Music (may be listened to or sung with a song leader "lining out" the words)
"How Majestic is Thy Name" & "You Are the One" by Keith Green

Opening Words of Praise (led by leader, congregation invited to repeat each line)
The Lord is my light and my salvation, whom shall I fear?
The Lord is the stronghold of my life; of whom shall I be afraid?
The Lord is my light and my salvation. I shall not be afraid

Song of Praise: "Praise God"
(words displayed on screen overhead or "lined out" by songleader; sung by congregation under leadership of songleader or praise singers)
Praise God, Praise God, Praise God in the morning, praise God in the noontime,
Praise God, Praise God, Praise God when the sun goes down
Serve God . . .
Love God . . .

Scripture Reading: 1 Corinthians 1:10–18

Thoughts on the Reading (message by pastor or worship leader)

Prayer of Response: "Lord, Be Glorified"
(words displayed on screen overhead; congregation singing under leadership of songleader or praise singers)
In our life, Lord, be glorified, be glorified,
In our life, Lord, be glorified today.

In Your Church, Lord, be unified, be unified,
In Your Church, Lord, be unified today.

89

Song of Praise: "Praise God"
(sung again with 1 or 3 verses, words displayed or "lined out")
Song of Response: "Bind Us Together, Lord"
(words displayed on screen overhead; congregational singing
led by songleader or music team)
Benediction (spoken by worship leader)
Go forth with the peace of Christ in your hearts and the unity
of God in your lives. Amen.

The Converted Seeker
Seeking in New Ways

"If you're looking to grow on this
journey, we'll walk with you."

The Converted Seeker refers to the Seeker who has sought
God, found the Holy One in an organized faith community
through one of your Seeker Services, and now yearns for more
conformity, tradition, and organization in his or her faith walk.
Many Converted Seekers are very likely already sitting in
church pews each Sunday morning. Several would-be converts
are probably also sitting there each week, hiding behind the
guise of "Follower" for fear of admitting their doubts and
questions. I believe that the Converted Seeker can often find
worship fulfillment in any of the previously discussed Seeker
services.

Some authors propose Seeker services that are primarily
ethical in nature with little reference to God, scripture, or
Christian heritage. The Church owes more to its Seekers than
another good ethics lesson. Most Seekers can turn to Public
Television for interesting debates on morality, usually more
completely presented than any worship service could hope to
offer.

Other church leaders propose that the "Seeker event" should provide an introduction to Christianity without any call to discipleship or invitation to faith maturity. Most Seekers come with a yearning to join a journey of faith that embraces their complex questions and invites them to wrestle as mature adults with the doubts that pervade the human situation. Additionally, Seekers can find inspiration and education in watching Followers respond to calls to discipleship or invitations to faith maturity.

Other Seeker services are nothing more than glorified "cheerleading" sessions for Jesus. But, the spiritual Seeker does not come to Christian worship for a motivational speech (which Dale Carnegie speakers or Amway conventions offer much more enthusiastically than most pastors can imagine).

The Seeker that the church can serve is the Seeker who searches for the Holy and often already engages in "God-talk." This Seeker is on a spiritual quest and open to spiritual writings such as the Holy Scriptures. Thus, even when this Seeker finds God or accepts Christ, the worship services we have designed can still challenge and broaden the spiritual journey of this Seeker. The Converted Seeker need not ever be obligated to attend traditional worship services or evangelical praise services in order to grow in faith and love of God and neighbor. The Seeker, though converted, may always be most comfortable in the service that blends the secular and the sacred. For this reason, a Seeker service need not be designed to negate or deny our religious beliefs, writings, or heritage. Rather, all Seeker services can integrate our religious traditions with the modern world in a way that is respectful of both the secular and the sacred. At the same time, Seeker services are constantly cognizant of the need to welcome those for whom the tradition is unfamiliar.

If a Seeker finds conversion during the spiritual journey in your church, the Seeker may yearn for more than worship can offer. This Seeker may request additional training in the religious heritage of your church, more in-depth study of Holy

Scriptures, or more challenging calls to live the faith. These yearnings are best handled in small group settings—short-term seminars and classes, ongoing study groups, Wesleyan-style class meetings,[6] or even support group settings. Worship is one part of the spiritual journey, not the whole and sum of the experience. Smaller, more intimate settings help the Seeker to know that we walk together on our journey of faith. Invite the Seeker to explore different routes on this journey, and the journey will carry the Seeker closer to the Holy One—fulfilling the search that began long before the Seeker ever entered the doors of the church.

Notes

1. Gill, Dennis. Quoted during Worship Class at Church Music Summer School, Perkins School of Theology, Southern Methodist University, Dallas, Texas. June 1997.

2. See Chapter 4, "Tools for the 21st Century" for details regarding language that welcomes and examples of how to incorporate such language.

3. Strawn, Betty. Quoted during Worship Class at Church Music Summer School, Perkins School of Theology, Southern Methodist University, Dallas, Texas. June 1997.

4. Portions of the worship services designated with an asterisk are reprinted from *The United Methodist Book of Worship*, Copyright 1992, The United Methodist Publishing House. All hymn and song texts are reprinted by right of public domain. Hymnal page numbers refer to *The United Methodist Hymnal*. All scripture quotes from The New Revised Standard Version of The Holy Bible.

5. Quote from the New Revised Standard Version of the Holy Bible.

6. Class meetings of 12 persons each met weekly to confess and examine the state of the class members' souls. These meetings were an intricate part of the Wesleyan Methodist

movement in 18th century England. In today's world, this emphasis on small accountability groups has again gained attention. Bill Easum refers to them as "LIFE Groups." Other authors use the term "cell structure" or "small group ministry" or "covenant groups." David Lowes Watson provides several helpful resources for small group ministries. Consult his book *Covenant Discipleship: Christian Formation through Mutual Accountability* (Nashville: Discipleship Resources, 1991) for more information on this style of ministry.

CHAPTER FOUR

Tools for the Twenty-first Century

As churches move into the twenty-first century, church leaders will need a variety of tools and resources to address the changing needs of Followers and Seekers. Worship services can become much more creative and innovative with the use of these resources. Other outreach opportunities are greatly enhanced when churches utilize the many resources available through computer usage, telephone capabilities, and other technological tools. Perhaps most importantly, the increasing availability of information makes it easier than ever for church leaders to understand who Seekers are, what the needs of Seekers are, and how Seekers might relate to Followers. Because we are living in an age of information and technology, resources already abound for church leaders and worship planners to access. However, the accessibility of these resources is somewhat debatable. Just try to perform a search on the Internet, and you will see what a challenge accessing information can be! Nevertheless, for those who are trying to minister with Seekers, accessing the available resources is essential.

In general, the best resources for reaching Seekers of younger generations are going to be found in the secular world. Television, computer games, resources on the World Wide Web, commercial radio, movies, best-selling books, and music videos can often provide the greatest means of understanding and reaching Seekers. Unfortunately, the church has not been a great leader in anticipating the changing situations and needs of society. As a seminary professor once said: "The Church is supposed to be the light of the world. Unfortunately, it has usually been the tail light." The church must turn all too often to the secular world for the leadership necessary to address the future before it becomes the distant past. Turning to secular resources does not mean buying into all of the values and agendas that such resources present. Rather, the church can incorporate the best of the secular world and the most useful tools society can provide while incorporating faith-centered values and goals focused on the gospel. Incorporating the best of the secular in order to evangelize the world for Christ is hardly a new idea! From Paul's exhortation to the Athenians as to the identity of their "unknown God" to St. Patrick's explanation that the woman whom the Irish venerated was really the virgin Mary, Christian history is full of church leaders who have made use of whatever resources were available to them in order to proclaim the good news.

Certainly, as Followers begin navigating through this "strange land" of addressing the needs of Seekers and designing worship experiences to reach Seekers, the tools for that navigation must be refined and used regularly. Such tools can become bridges that span the distance that so many Followers feel from Seekers. As the bridges become more accessible and stable, Seekers and Followers will be better able to cross into each other's worlds and relate to each other on their common spiritual journeys.

Media Resources

One of the quickest ways to begin understanding the influences on Seekers is to follow the media. Follow the media regularly, but take everything you have learned with a grain of salt. Media resources are heavily influenced by advertisers, Hollywood's love of itself, and exaggeration of societal interests. Nevertheless, Hollywood, advertisers, and the media tend to cater to public tastes, so the information gained there can be helpful when observed with a critical eye. The savvy observer can find ways of sifting through the media portrayal and finding grains of truth in the midst of the hype.

Television is perhaps the most widespread reflection of, and commentary on, American society. The rise of cable television programs, led by the FOX network, is particularly relevant when dealing with Generation X (Busters) or the Millennial Generation (Birthers). FOX network programming is strong and intentional in attracting those generations. The intense fascination with the para-normal in shows like "The X Files" and "Millennium" tells us much about the issues that young adults are pondering and discussing. Shows like "The Simpsons" and "Beavis and Butt-head" that explode stereotypes about the nuclear family and everyday behavior are equally helpful in understanding the attitudes of younger Seekers.

Even traditional network programming reveals interesting insights into the views and interests of American viewers. "Friends," one of the most popular Generation X shows, offers a glimpse into the loneliness and isolation that so many young adults feel in the early years away from home. This show also wrestles with the ways in which many Xers address those feelings and situations. For Generation Xers and possibly for the Millennial Generation, marriage occurs later in life and careers start on a slower path than in previous generations. Likewise, career decisions are often delayed by the vast array of choices that young adults face. The stability in social networks that long-term employment and marital relationships provide is not something most people encounter today in their early adult years. Thus, isolation and loneliness will be key issues for the church to address in both programming and worship planning. Certainly, Jesus' teachings offer much hope and many guides for community-building to address that type of disconnection in modern society. "Mad About You" goes to the next step in young adult lives, as the characters face the first steps of marriage and creating a family. They struggle with the early divorce of friends around them as well as the envy of their single friends. They also face the challenges of balancing career with family, all in the context of trying to fulfill a lifetime commitment that they have made to one another. On the heavier side, shows like *ER* and *NYPD Blue* look at the stresses of working in high pressured institutions, while trying to carve out a life in the midst of complex choices and relationships. For young people today, encountering complexity and disarray in relationships and society is becoming commonplace. Older adults also find shows such as these compelling, as they too try to deal with the quickly changing world where "old world" values like strictly-defined gender roles and racial segregation are no longer acceptable. *NYPD Blue* has captured this issue compellingly in the character of Andy Sipowicz. Andy is an aging police detective who has difficulty balancing his traditional values with modern day pressures. His "Archie Bunker" attitudes often bump up against the more modern-day opinions of his wife and his patrol partner, both of whom reject prejudicial values and stereotypes. Sipowicz contrasts strongly with the younger characters, who seem perfectly comfortable in the diverse and complex world they encounter on a daily basis.

Made-for-television movies are particularly fascinating because of their obsession with "true life" stories. It is as if *The National Inquirer* has found a niche in the television market. Of course, these movies would not be produced if they didn't attract viewers. Society's overt fascination with the tragedies and horrors of our world may seem disgusting, yet it points to a confusion about morality and values. Such fascination also exemplifies peoples' need for direction and guidance in addressing the complex decisions that persons must face in this day and age. "True-to-life" series like *Cops* and dramatic news magazines like *A Current Affair* point to similar interests and concerns amongst American viewers. None of these trends can be taken lightly by church leaders who want to relate to Seekers, nor can they simply be dismissed from the pulpit as "sinful" or a "waste of time" if preachers expect to be relevant. Because of our avoidance in addressing these issues in worship and Christian education settings, even Christians have very few non-secular choices for information-gathering and moral development. For instance, you would be hard-pressed to find a Christian book that addresses the difficult issues of raising children who have become violent or promiscuous. Christian literature that addresses controversial issues all too often becomes a platform for the author to preach judgment. For Seekers (and for most Followers), religious writings on today's life concerns are more helpful when they become an invitation for Christians to dialogue and explore the complexity of the issues at hand. Much Christian literature even seems to pretend that current realities like police brutality, racial violence, sexual addictions, food disorders, domestic violence, and ongoing marital infidelity are non-existent in the Christian world. Seekers and Followers know that these realities exist, and pretenses to the contrary only drive a deeper wedge between the secular and the sacred aspects of our lives.

Radio provides another avenue of access to the world of the Seeker. Talk radio has changed significantly, led by characters like Rush Limbaugh and Howard Stern. Recently, I have been listening to "Dr. Laura" on a local radio station. She hosts a syndicated advice-talk show. However, Ann Landers she is not! Dr. Laura's advice is sharp and biting, judgmental and clear-cut. Although she claims to be an "opinion talk show host" rather than an advisor, she offers her opinions as advice and commands. Even though her doctorate is in physiology, she gladly offers psychological, theological, and moral opinions hour after hour. There are no "gray" areas for Dr. Laura, and her listeners seem to believe everything she advises with little or no objection. As I listen to the callers on the air, many of whom are under the age of 30, I am saddened by our willingness to follow without questioning. And yet, I think it comes not because we are looking at an upcoming generation of blind followers, but because we are looking at a lonely generation of adults. Her listeners seem to have little if any biological family support and few opportunities for value-centered dialogue in friendship and work circles. Although Dr. Laura claims to advise from a Christian perspective, she attracts listeners who seem to have little trust in the church as a relevant or accessible place for guidance and nurture. If the church begins to open its doors to Seekers in relevant and non-judgmental ways, talk show hosts like Dr. Laura will find their popularity ratings decreasing as they are no longer needed.

Radio is also an excellent entry-point into the world of music for the Seekers you wish to attract. A call to the marketing department of local radio stations will guide you in finding the radio stations that appeal to the age or demographic group you are called to serve. Music for the Seekers of the next two generations is not likely to be anything like the praise music that has pervaded so much of the church growth movement in the last 20 years. Whether the young adults in your community listen to gangsta' rap, alternative rock, Seattle grunge, young country, heavy metal, techno jazz, revived "soft metal" (rock groups Boston or Foreigner), or the new form of folk rock that has gained popularity in the 90s, the music of young adults is complex and challenging. Live music will continue to be the best means of providing musical leadership in the church, but the challenges for finding those musicians will increase considerably. The music that young adults listen to currently is light years beyond the "pop" music that church leaders have been utilizing in praise services for the last 20 years. Most church musicians are simply not prepared for the musical demands of the upcoming generations. Fortunately, the quality of performance need not be as slick or perfect as was necessary for Boomers. For Xers and Millennials, music emphasis is likely to focus on authenticity, enjoyment of performing, diversity of styles, and relevance of lyrics. Thus, volunteer and professional musicians who are willing to learn new musical styles will have many opportunities to minister with Seekers of these younger generations. With younger Seekers, the "excellence" previously required of musicians, classical or pop, seems to be less important than genuine compassion and interest for the music and the listener.

Newspapers and magazines are chock full of articles on younger generations. As we approach the turn of the millennium, do not look for this trend to change. Reading everything available will enhance your understanding of where people are hurting, why people are making certain choices, and how people are being portrayed in the media. Again, a savvy eye for bias is needed when reading these materials. If we fall into the trap of trusting the printed word without analysis and some skepticism, we will find that conclusions are not always accurate. For instance, in the early 1990s, when I first began studying the demographics on Generation X, newspapers and magazines were quick to tell me of the negative situation of this group of young people. Articles were full of depressing stories about gang violence, suicide rates, financial struggles, and a general failure to succeed. Contrastingly, almost all American news magazines in 1997 have included at least one article applauding the entrepreneurial spirit of this up and coming generation. Now, the media seems pleased to applaud the challenge this diverse group offers to the marketing profession. Synthesizing information, while filtering out media stereotypes, thus becomes the task and challenge of church leaders who wish to address the hurts of the modern world. Integrating this information becomes a part of the mission for those of us who want to help persons make decisions for Christ and define themselves in relationship to God.

For me, movies are a particularly enjoyable way to access the interests and concerns of Seekers. As mentioned earlier, an increased fascination with the spiritual began to be seen in movies of the early 80s (*Ghost* and even the *Star Wars* trilogy). This spiritual interest is on the rise, but taking different twists in more recent movies. Angels receive very human portrayals (*Michael* and *The Preacher's Wife*). People experience eternal life through the humans they have touched before death rather than through some heavenly experience *(Phenomenon* and *Flatliners).* Seekers are contemplating serious moral questions like the death penalty *(Dead Man Walking* and *The Chamber),* racism and race-related violence *(Boyz N the Hood* and *A Time to Kill),* and the close relationship between evil and good *(Interview with the Vampire* and *Dracula).* Although watching movies like these might offend some people's Christian sensitivities, such exposure offers pastors and Christian educators compelling sermon illustrations and valuable insights into the means by which people are addressing these issues. Again, movies are the product of Hollywood, not the common consumer, but they have a heavy influence on consumers and do reflect the interests and concerns that appeal to our culture.

Technology

In addition to noting these more "traditional" forms of media, church leaders for the twenty-first century will need to invest some time and money in understanding today's technology. Accessing the information available through computers is essential when working with young Seekers. With the help of the young adults in the church, older leaders can become familiar with chat rooms, email, and other on-line services. Accessing the Internet and learning how to navigate the Web will not only help church leaders understand the lifestyle of many Seekers, but it also provides a vast array of information for Followers to absorb. Information management is also essential, as you will quickly discover. The sheer volume of information can quickly become a hindrance rather than a tool if you do not have a means of selecting, storing, and eventually integrating the useful information.

In addition to information access, computers provide a helpful tool in understanding how many young Seekers invest their time and money. Computers, stereos, televisions, VCRs, and other technological advances are a common part of many Seekers' lives. If the church continues to rely on outdated and inadequate equipment, young Seekers may dismiss the church as "out of touch" with modern society. Additionally, Seekers and Followers who wish to share their gifts as church volunteers will need access to the church via modern communication tools. Busy volunteers need to know that they can communicate with their church via fax or email. Innovative worship planners like to know that the church has appropriate equipment for the music and video ideas that they bring to the worship planning tables. Some Seekers will even make their first church contact through a church Web page or email correspondence!

The rise in individualistic-style group games is also closely related to the available technology of the day. On-line computer games, interactive CD-ROM games, laser tag, and paintball are only the beginning of a changing approach to entertainment and game-playing. Before passing judgment, church leaders are well advised to experiment with some of these technological toys. Before I left Detroit, my "girlfriend gang" took me out for a last "girls' night out." We went downtown to the tourist section known as "Greektown" for dining and window shopping. While window shopping, one of my friends said "Oh, they have laser tag! Let's go in for a game." In typically prudish fashion, I said "No, friends. I'm a pacifist. I don't do guns or violence." They begged, cajoled, and eventually coaxed me into the game room. We formed our own team and played against a group of teens who massacred us with their lasers as they prepared for a tournament the next day. By the time we finished, my friends had to drag me away from the incredibly fun game! No, I am not advocating an increase in violent game-playing for pastors. But I did realize that I needed to walk in their shoes before condemning. I found in our 30-minutes of darkness and laser lights that I was able to play out a lot of tension and anger I was feeling about leaving my home and my friends, while also relieving some anxiety about the changes I was facing. The game turned out not to be as pointless or as evil as I would have judged prior to playing. As I watched the youth playing against us, I thought about their other alternates for entertainment that evening in downtown Detroit. Clearly, they were participating in one of the best options available to them.

Human Contact

"Maybe it is more the *people*, rather than the *format* that makes the critical difference [in reaching Seekers]."
Terry Heislen, St. Mark United Methodist Church, McAllen, Texas

Which brings me to the most important tool for working with Seekers. In order to reach out to and minister with Seekers, Followers must spend time with the people churches plan to serve. In visiting the hangouts of the generation of Seekers you are striving to serve, you will develop relationships and understandings that will provide the seeds and foundation of a Seeker-oriented ministry. Radio station advertisements can often help in directing you toward those hangouts. Restaurants, coffee houses, movie theaters, house parties, dance clubs, Raves, schools, and college cafe's are all helpful starting points in working with younger Seekers, but each community will differ.

If you are striving to reach Seekers in their senior citizen years, consider retirement apartments or senior centers as places for outreach and dialogue. Persons in this stage of life are not necessarily churched, but they most definitely are facing challenging theological issues as the majority of their friends and loved ones die. Those seniors still living begin to contemplate the meaning of the lives they have lived and the deaths they will one day die. At they same time, they are also trying to cope with the loneliness that the death of so many friends brings to their lives. Baby Boomer Seekers are often found in parenting groups, country clubs, health and fitness clubs, lunch spots, bars near their workplaces, or on camping trips in National and State Parks. Assuming some of your own church members participate in secular events and organizations, Followers can provide a wonderful wealth of information. Followers of the generation of Seekers for whom you are searching are one of your best resources in understanding Seekers.

Working with Seekers involves a good amount of detective work. However, these are not persons who are hiding from the church. Once a few Seekers in a community know that you are seeking them in a genuine and caring fashion, those Seekers will bring other Seekers into your presence. When you begin spending time with Seekers, listen, listen, listen. . . . Ministry with today's Seekers is much more of a "Jesus-modeled" ministry than a ministry modeled after Martin Luther or John Calvin or even the Pope. Effective ministry with Seekers begins with a question, continues with a great deal of listening, and often ends with a story to evoke more questions. Advice-giving and simplistic guidance will only provide short-lived successes with Seekers, for most Seekers are willing to struggle in the search for answers. The church, however, can provide perimeters and support in the struggle.

Using the Tools We Have

For many churches, your greatest tool in reaching Seekers may be your current worship service and current church leadership. Not all churches seem irrelevant and outdated to Seekers. But, before you assume you are one of the relevant ones, take a hard look around.

Atmosphere

What kind of atmosphere does your worship space provide? Is your sanctuary warm and inviting, accessible and comfortable, well-lit, and moderately temperatured? Do entry areas move people toward the worship space and offer directions to classrooms, offices, childcare, and bathrooms? Are current churchgoers friendly, but not overwhelming, to newcomers? Do worship leaders portray friendly attitudes and inviting language? Are participants welcome to arrive late and leave early? Do worship participants have plenty of space for parking and seating? Is the worship space full enough to provide a sense of excitement and energy? Positive answers to these questions indicate a crucial tool in reaching Seekers. Even in the most traditional church, many Seekers will find a warm and inviting atmosphere more important than any other single factor. Because of the increasing problem of loneliness and isolation in our society, warm and inclusive worship and social opportunities can be some of the most successful experiences in reaching Seekers. The offering of hospitality is a valuable gift to Seekers, many of whom do not find the world a very hospitable place.

Music

If yours is a church filled with diverse musical talents, you have one of the greatest resources available in ministering to Seekers. Using a variety of musical selections and styles throughout the service can help to compensate for a worship service that may seem too traditional for effective ministry with Seekers. Many Seekers, particularly of the Millennial Generation, will tolerate traditional worship when the music is accessible and moving. Jazzing up old hymns with drums and syncopated rhythm can be a very effective part of Seeker worship—for any age group. Simply adding a trumpet or violin to the melody line, or accompanying the choir on flute can provide beauty and warmth that inspires Seekers to listen more openly. If you currently offer a praise service that includes a talented praise band, your musicians may be well-prepared to offer some diversity in their musical leadership. Adding a popular secular song on the theme of the day, or a newly composed song by the band may be a first step toward reaching younger Seekers with a praise service. Looking outside your current musical leadership may also reveal a number of Followers who are capable and willing to offer alternative musical leadership for a Seeker-oriented worship service.

Order and Flow of the Worship Service

Worship services that flow naturally and in a common direction are always more comprehensible to a visitor than disjointed services. So many of our worship services are full of "interruptions," such as announcements or collecting the offering or waiting for a musician to come running back in from a duty in the Sunday School. You may be tempted to think, "well most folks are used to commercials, so what's the problem?!" Just ask a television commercial advertiser, and you'll discover that keeping people on the station when the commercial begins is a challenging task. Most persons are fond of "channel surfing," particularly during the commercial breaks . . . and few of our worship interruptions are clever enough to prevent a similar "mind surfing" on the part of our sister and brother worshippers. Reviewing worship services with a team of critical eyes can help worship planners to find those interruptions. Then, the team can develop ways of either minimizing interruptions, clumping them together, or turning them into worthwhile parts of the worship service and flow.

For example, one of my churches had a 5–7 minute Mission Moment scheduled in the worship service, presented by a very inspiring speaker. She represented a community service agency supported by the church, and people looked forward to hearing from her. In any circumstance, her words would have been compelling. However, in this case, the unexpected death of a church member, Mel, who was one of the agency's most dedicated volunteers turned her Mission Moment into a Moment of Inspiration. She framed her entire message in terms of Mel's life and ministry. By doing so, she helped us to see the people serviced by that agency through Mel's eyes and encouraged us to see his commitment as a role model for our church. Her Mission Moment was truly a commercial that no one was tempted to "surf" past! Likewise, offerings can be presented openly and honestly with words about the meaning of giving and receiving used to introduce the time of collection. Offerings may be presented as a response to special Mission Moments like the one discussed above, or as a response to the message for the day. For Seekers, as well as for all of the church guests on a given Sunday, the offering needs to be introduced in a non-obligatory manner. A simple introduction could be: "This worship service is our gift to you, so please do not look at this time of offering as a time to pay for this freely-given gift. Rather, this time of offering is an opportunity for persons who wish to share their gifts or respond to God's blessings with financial support of the church to do so. Please enjoy the musical offering shared during this time as another part of our gift to you this morning." Liewise, offering music need not be "throwaway music," but rather can be presented as an example of self-giving to the community and returning of our gifts to God.

Most importantly, however, the flow of the service needs to be intentionally planned. Rather than creating stagnant ponds or frustrating whirlpools, careful worship planners can create a flowing river or a rushing stream of rapids. Whether the service be slow and meditative, methodical and predictable, or spontaneous and exuberant, the service needs to go somewhere. What is the theme for the day? What mood is the Holy Spirit trying to convey? What message is arising from the scriptures for the service? Every aspect of the service should build to a certain point, whether that point comes in the middle or at the end of the service. As with good literature, a well-planned worship service takes the participants on a journey. The journey needs to be intentional and purposeful if we expect Seekers (and Followers) to return week after week. As my Creative Writing teacher used to say, "What is the point?" The careful worship planner can answer that question regarding each worship service. Worship planners must not only know the overarching theology and mission of worship that guides their work, but they must also determine and know what the goal of a given worship service is. Of course, the Holy Spirit is mysterious enough that our most carefully-planned goals will often become very different in implementation. Naturally, this does not mean that God wants us to simply sit around and hope that the Holy Spirit shows up each Sunday morning to create purpose out of a disjointed and poorly-planned worship service. God deserves and demands our best efforts, and Seekers are not likely to be impressed by Followers who do not take their ministry of worship seriously enough to give it their best.

Theme and Deliverance of God's Word

As you review your current worship service or begin planning new worship services, ask yourself whether the theme of today's service or today's message (sermon) can be written in one sentence. My seminary preaching professor required this of each sermon we wrote, and the self-discipline required to find the theses of my sermons has improved my preaching considerably! Worship services need to be held to the same level of accountability, with the goal that the themes of both the message and the worship service are somewhat similar! Developing this kind of thematic approach, even in the lectionary-based church, will enhance the abilities of all persons involved in worship planning and leadership. It will also help Seekers to understand the worship experience, even the parts that may seem mysterious or incomprehensible.

One of the new Followers in the church I serve said to me one morning, "I just realized today that Christ's body was broken by me and for me!" I pondered what she might be talking about, so I asked her to explain further. She could not remember what I had said, but she thought that something in my Words of Institution for Holy Communion had caught her ear. I asked if perhaps it was the message beforehand that evoked this thought, since the message had been on conflict and reconciliation within our church. She thought about it, and said, "Well, maybe, but I think it was something you said from the Communion Table." That evening, I tried to piece together what I might have said, since I usually improvise the Words of Institution to *fit the theme of the day's message!* Ah, I should have known. . . . I had indeed said something about our participation in breaking the Body of Christ and the promise that we were forgiven in Christ's breaking of his own Body. Just keeping the theme at the forefront of my mind as I led the service had helped the message to come alive in a new way for one of the worshippers.

The Written Word

In most Protestant churches today, Followers assume a certain amount of knowledge about the use of the written word. We hand out programs or bulletins with all kinds of cryptic messages and coded symbols. Even in many praise services, overhead transparencies assume a knowledge of when to repeat a chorus and when to move on to a new verse. Hymnals can be even more confusing! Taking a good look at the written materials in a church is a necessity if church leaders wish to reach Seekers. Do the worship bulletins explain any symbols used? What do those asterisks mean anyway? How small is the print that explains what they mean? Do participants know when they are invited to speak with other worshippers and leaders, or do they have to wait for someone else to tell them? Can people find the words for memorized parts of the service? Nothing is more embarrassing than having dozens of people forge ahead into a prayer or creed, leaving a Seeker behind in the dust. Our written materials need to explain what is coming next, how to participate fully and appropriately, and what physical actions might be required in such participation. Yes, most of these instructions will need to be repeated orally and modeled by the worship leaders, but the written program is worse than useless if it does not reflect clear-cut and simple guidance for participation in worship. If the service relies on overhead transparencies for song lyrics, then those same transparencies need to provide the words for memorized prayers and creeds that will be part of the worship experience.

Likewise, newsletters and informational brochures need to be accessible and understandable to Seekers. Using initials to advertise a small group or an event in the church is exclusive and, therefore, harmful in trying to reach Seekers. Inviting persons to a "potluck" dinner without explaining what "potluck" means and whether persons can attend who did not bring a dish to pass is not an invitation to Seekers.

In all of the written materials, a limited number of print fonts and the largest print font possible are helpful tools in making the materials readable and enjoyable. In particular, for older Seekers and Followers (meaning anyone who might need bifocals), having large print resources readily available helps Seekers to avoid the embarrassment of admitting that they could not read the materials provided.

Of course, the written materials must be available. When ushers go to sit with their families five minutes into the worship service and take the remaining programs or bulletins with them, late-coming Seekers will never see the perfect written resource you have created! When new families arrive and are never told that children's worship packets are sitting on a table in the back, the packets are non-existent for them. When informational brochures sit on a literature rack squeezed between dusty copies of devotional pamphlets and child abuse hotline flyers, the brochures are not providing information to the folks who need that information.

On the other hand, well-designed written materials that are shared with all who walk into the church's doors can be long-lasting tools of invitation and reference for Seekers. Weeks or even months later, Seekers will find that program or brochure and remember the experience of visiting a worshipping community. The goal for church leaders is to provide a memory that is pleasant and information that helps to connect that memory to the Seeker's ongoing journey.

Written Language That Welcomes Does *Not* Include

- Unexplained abbreviations (L. & C. For "Leader" and "Congregation," UMW for United Methodist Women, UCC for United Church of Christ)
- Unexplained symbols or codes ("Why are those words bolded?" the Seeker asks.)
- Unexplained ancient titles (Gloria Patri, Doxology)
- Undefined words unique to church publishing (for instance, "bulletin," "acolyte," "liturgist," "introit," "sanctuary," "narthex," "chancel")
- Printed instructions that are incomplete (such as a heading for "The Lord's Prayer" without the words of the Prayer printed out)

Written Language That Welcomes *Does* Include

- Printed instructions for movement during the service (Communion Procedure, when to sit or stand)
- Printed instructions for utilizing worship resources during the service (page numbers for Bible readings, registration instructions, where to find hymnals or songbooks)
- Names of worship leaders to help Seekers connect with a "real person."
- Pertinent church information, including phone numbers and addresses
- Invitations to upcoming church events

Language and Communication

Just as with the written word, our spoken word and non-verbal cues during worship can go a long way to creating warm memories and relevant connections. Language during worship needs to be inclusive in the best sense of the word. Being inclusive is not merely an issue of political correctness; it is an issue of representing God and the Church in a holistic manner. As mentioned in an earlier chapter, inclusive does not refer simply to neutered pronouns. For Seekers, inclusive means rich imagery, welcoming attitudes, and comfortable diversity. Our worship language needs to convey a message that all who enter the church doors are not only welcome, but are seen as children of God who have accepted an open invitation into Christ's presence.

Communication during the service needs to be clear and relaxed. Trying to impress people with our theological expertise or liturgical knowledge will only drive Seekers further away from the church as Seekers pursue the spiritual journey. Many of the suggestions and questions addressed in the issues related to written communication are duplicated in the issue of spoken communication. Using acronyms, abbreviated names, and unexplained church-specific words is a quick way to exclude Seekers from our midst. On the other hand, worship leaders who invite persons to the "women's group discussion on parenting teenagers" are clearly communicating something the church has to offer. Pastors who remind persons that their written prayer requests will receive daily prayers from several members of the congregation are inviting Seekers to be supported by this community of faith.

Non-verbal communication is perhaps even more essential. Seeing worship leaders with crossed arms, scowling faces, slumped shoulders, or stressed fists makes any worshipper uncomfortable. For Seekers, these non-verbal cues can become representative of the entire church. On the other hand, warm handshakes, shy smiles, twinkling eyes, and open body positions display an attitude of invitation and comfort. In my husband's church, many of the Followers are embarrassed by their worship leader who begins the service each week. John wears his jogging suit or shorts and golf shirt each week. He stands in a casual pose, often beginning his announcements with a silly joke, accompanied by his crooked smirk and twinkling eyes, before he invites people to greet one another. By the time he is finished, even the most uncomfortable Seeker is likely to feel safe enough to share a handshake or a smile with the many people who approach during the time of greeting. Because of this comfortable atmosphere that has been created, many Followers are exuberant and confident in their willingness to approach visitors and offer a greeting. Indeed, John's non-verbal communications are the key to his success . . . even when his jokes fall flat or his announcements become scrambled.

Here Is the Steeple

Church-owned properties, along with property available to Followers in the church, can be valuable resources as new ministries with Seekers are initiated. Often, alternate spaces for Seeker worship are readily available once church leaders begin to think beyond the limits of a traditional sanctuary. One of the most meaningful programs I have seen in local church outreach to Seekers depends heavily on the use of the neighboring elementary school's gym every Thursday evening. The church can reach out to its neighborhood children and families, by providing food, fellowship and lesson time in the church building and recreation time in the school building next door. The elementary school, in turn, has use of additional parking spaces in the church's parking lot during the week and a better access route for its school buses each week day. The relationship between school and church has been beneficial to both institutions without crossing any of the legal lines separating church and state.

Church Talk That Welcomes

- Welcome to this time of worship and praise to God!
  Not: Will you stand and join in the Call to Worship . . .
- This is the way to the worship room (or auditorium).
  Not: Worship is in the sanctuary.
- Please join us for coffee and snacks in the lobby!
  Not: Fellowship time follows in the narthex.
- If you would like a church tour, please come to the front platform (or stage) area after our worship service this morning.
  Not: Church tours will begin at the chancel after church.
- I would like to invite John to the podium to tell us his story.
  Not: John will be filling the pulpit this morning.
- You will find the order of events for this worship service printed in the program you received as you entered this morning.
  Not: Please turn in your bulletin to the Invocation.
- Our worship reader will now lead us in prayer.
  Not: Our liturgist will now lead us in prayer.
- We wish to express a special thank you today to all the children who serve as candle lighters for us each week! OR Thank you to all of you children who light our candles each week, reminding us that God's loving light is always present in our lives!
  Not: Thank you, acolytes, for your service to our church.
- Thank you, choir, for that beautiful song calling us into God's presence this morning!
  Not: The choir will now sing our morning Introit.
- We now come to that time in the service when we offer all of your prayers to God, prayers of joy and concern from God's people.
  Not: Please join me in the Bidding Prayers.
- Those who are able are invited to stand as we sing our Song of Praise and Thanksgiving to God.
  Not: Please stand for the Doxology.

In a different vein, one of the struggling Detroit churches has utilized its "city block" of building ownership to open a justice-oriented art museum and a non-profit clothing store. Both businesses cater widely to Seekers in the community, making the church much more viable and effective in its outreach efforts.

A Puget Sound church in Washington makes frequent use of one of its church member's waterfront properties. The old family lodge, known as Camp Coleman, serves well as a small retreat center or a gathering spot for dinners and recreational events.

Within each church building, there are often many other tangible properties that can be valuable in enhancing a creative worship ministry. Most pastors would be surprised to find the plethora of theater costumes, musical instruments, and audio-visual resources collecting dust in the various closets of the church building. Often, women's groups or education work areas are the best sleuths in locating these resources for inventory so that all church leaders can be aware of resources available at their fingertips.

Open the Doors and There Are the People

Far and above any other tool your church may have in reaching Seekers, human resources are still the most valuable. In many churches, there are artists, dancers, and musicians whose skills have not been tapped because the style of their artistic training is so very different from the style traditionally utilized in the church. These artists, alongside current participants and leaders in the music and drama ministries of the church, can be very helpful tools in reaching Seekers.

Many Followers have usable skills that are not being utilized by church leaders. Marketing specialists and advertising experts can help church leaders to reach certain groups of Seekers effectively and appropriately. Organizers and secretaries can be very helpful in addressing the increased administrative load of a church that is successfully reaching Seekers. Public speakers can be resources as worship leaders and motivational speakers, particularly when they are willing to share personal testimonies of their own faith journeys.

Often when churches begin looking at human resources, churches forget to look outside the church walls. Each church has inactive church members, community leaders, community artists, and Followers in other faith communities who are heavily invested in seeing the church perform its ministry successfully and effectively. These persons can be valuable resources, particularly as a church looks toward reaching Seekers. Many of the community leaders and artists who are most invested in seeing a local church serve the community are themselves Seekers. These community leaders can offer helpful insights into the needs and interests of Seekers in the particular community where they live and serve. Calling on these leaders and artists can be an excellent way of enhancing the church's ministry and connecting with Seekers.

Finally, the "worker bees" of a church are incredible resources for developing new ministries with Seekers. Every church is filled with people who pray, people who work hard, and people who care. In reaching Seekers, the ministry must be undergirded with an enormous amount of prayer. Searching for those persons who have the gift of intercession or prayer is a worthwhile task if church leaders want to reach Seekers. Often, some of the homebound members of a church have developed great disciplines for daily prayer.

Diligent workers become the backbone of any new ministry. If a new Seeker-ministry is staffed only with artists and leaders, it will be riddled with conflict and ill preparation. Diligent workers help to balance the ego-needs of strong leaders and to organize the creative spirit of artistic thinkers.

People who care, however, are the real key to success in ministry with Seekers. Seekers will be touched most effectively if they connect with Followers who care. Caring is not something that can be forced or even trained—although skills for showing how much one cares can be taught. Caring and loving concern arise from the heart, and Seekers will know when they have connected with Followers who genuinely care about them and their faith journey. Such authentic love and interest are increasingly rare in our society, and very much the kind of love and interest that Jesus modeled for all Seekers and Followers during his ministry on earth. As Jesus discovered, Followers who care will not have to look for the needs. The needs will come to Followers who care. When your Seeker ministry has begun to attract persons who never saw an advertisement, you will know that ministry of love and care has now taken on a life of its own. Such love and care spread like the fire of the Holy Spirit, changing lives and drawing people toward the flame. Such love and care are *the* essential tool for ministry with Seekers and Followers.

Assessing the Tools

These are tools that every church has, even if you have to look for them. The question church leaders must address is "How well are we reaching people with the tools that we have?" As leaders assess this question, they will note the need to sharpen some tools and replace others. Church leaders will probably have to add new tools to the church's toolbox as well. When assessing the tools, it is also important to recognize that no one church can reach every Seeker or Follower who comes through the doors. A little self-honesty is helpful as church leaders acknowledge that the tools being used may not reach every Seeker. The recognition that Seekers are reachable can help to determine what shape the toolbox needs to be in if the church is to be a place where Seekers and Followers can journey and work together.

As your church begins to explore its toolbox, you may find that many aspects of your worship and outreach experience are already reaching Seekers. Still other aspects may be readily adaptable to reach even more. Yet, even with many Seeker-friendly aspects, you may find that Seekers drift into your lives and drift away after a short period of time. Although this may be a necessary part of a certain Seeker's spiritual journey, too often the Seeker drifts away because the Seeker has not found spiritual depth or assistance on the journey of faith. Most often, journeys of faith bring Seekers into our midst. Thus, we will want to offer the spiritual depth and assistance necessary for Seekers to travel with Followers on an ongoing basis. Seekers and Followers turn to the church for guidance and direction, and much of that guidance and direction comes from the pulpit or podium. When the message coming from the preacher is comprehensible, offering practical guidance or direction, many Seekers will find in the church a wonderful place for spiritual growth and fulfillment. After assessing the impact of the worship messages and message formats, some worship teams may want to explore innovative ways of further increasing the effectiveness of the worship message. With each improved tool, more Seekers can be reached and more Followers and Seekers will find their spiritual journeys meaningful and worthwhile.

CHAPTER FIVE

Preaching to a New Generation

The preached and proclaimed word has long been a central part of Protestant worship. It has also been one of the most controversial and personal parts of worship. Ask ten worshippers what makes a good sermon, and you will likely receive ten different answers. Certainly, preaching styles have changed over the centuries. From the Reformation style of preaching doctrine and theological treatises to the early American camp-meeting style of preaching fire and brimstone, preaching has varied as much as any other aspect of Christian worship.

Even today, preaching is hardly limited to one style. In some churches, the sermon takes the form of an extended Bible lesson, or exegesis of the text. Listeners spend their worshipping time reading scripture passages as the preacher explains Greek and Hebrew word origins and theological underpinnings of the various passages. Or, the preacher takes listeners through a passage verse by verse to guide listeners in understanding God's will for living on a daily basis . . . God's will as defined by the preacher.

In another setting, the sermon may be much like those Reformation sermons: an intellectual exercise in theological terms and their meaning for Christians. Listeners are required to pay careful attention to the theological twists and turns and the academic language as the preacher takes the listeners through a journey of intellectual pursuit. This pursuit intends

119

to draw the listener into a deeper understanding of who God is and how we might relate to God through Christ.

In yet another contemporary setting, the sermon may be little more than a motivational speech, helping listeners feel better about themselves or develop skills for living more ethical and holistic lives. Listeners are invited to remember a series of helpful hints or chronological points as the preacher explains the hows and whys of better Christian living. Often, the helpful hints are accompanied by a smattering of scripture verses from various parts of the Bible.

In some settings, the sermon may be a protracted lament on the difficulties of living in today's world, juxtaposed with a glimpse of the heavenly hope of a trouble-free and joyous afterlife. In these settings, listeners are often encouraged to strive for that hopeful attitude here on earth, in order to grasp a more optimistic outlook on the present. As listeners yearn for a better life here and now, they draw their deepest excitement from anticipating the best life of all: the heavenly life where "we'll eat pie in the sky, in the sweet by and by, after we die."

Or, as is increasingly the case, the sermon may be a time of relating theological themes or biblical stories to the Christian journey of a contemporary person. Here, listeners are encouraged to deepen their theological and biblical knowledge, while also being challenged to live out this knowledge on a regular basis.

In any of these cases, many sermons assume a great deal of familiarity with Christian language and with the art of preaching. Listeners are usually expected to understand the basics of Christian faith and to accept the uniqueness of the sermon experience. When developing a preaching style with Seekers, such assumptions and expectations are counter productive. Although there is certainly no set method of preaching for Seekers, there are ways of adapting current methods and developing new styles that will be more effective than current preaching styles.

Sermons Based on What?

Although arguments abound as to whether sermons should be biblically- or topically-based, Seekers are not as concerned with the subject matter of the sermon as they are with the sermon's relevance to their lives. Whether the preacher begins with assigned lections for the day, a topic of burning interest, or a biblical passage that has captured the preacher's attention, the sermon or message-time needs to be relevant and practical.

Relevant and practical sermons need not be shallow and secular! Many preachers who began early in the praise service movement learned the hard way that sermons preached without a biblical or theological foundation quickly degenerate into motivational pep talks, nothing more. As Followers, church leaders are challenged to invite Seekers onto the Christian journey. But in our rush to invite Seekers, we should take care that the journey is indeed a Christian one. For this reason, all of my sermons are biblically based, and most of my sermons are even lectionary-based. I have found that the discipline of connecting the biblical story to daily life has enhanced my sermon-writing and has improved my own abilities as a pastor and preacher. Whatever material preachers utilize when preaching to Seekers, the message needs to help people connect their spiritual journeys and their daily lives; and it needs to do this on an ongoing basis.

One way of preaching relevant sermons is to parallel biblical illustrations with secular stories, or by pointing out a theological example in a popular movie. Another way of preaching practical sermons is to challenge people to live in a specific way or to strive for a specific change of heart as they live their daily lives. The preacher can illustrate the pragmatic character of sermons by holding himself or herself accountable to the lesson of the day. Testimonies from Followers or even Seekers about a personal change or challenge in response to the biblical message can be even more effective in reaching listeners. As people begin to see the practical outcome of hearing

121

and studying God's word, Seekers and Followers are more likely to listen and learn more diligently.

Judge Not, Lest Ye Be Judged

Message-time with Seekers is not the time to preach your best fire and brimstone sermon. Seekers are not looking for judgment or dictatorial leaders. Seekers are looking for traveling companions and companion-guides to shepherd them through the difficult stages of the spiritual journey. Thus, the most effective messages or sermons with Seekers are non-judgmental.

This does not mean, however, that preachers need to be non-committal or wishy-washy in the proclamation of God's word. It simply means that as we explore the biblical story, we need to be honest about our own shortcomings and confusions. For example, listeners can learn that marriage requires commitment without being misled into thinking that the preacher is a perfect spouse. Hearing the preacher admit to the challenges she or he faces in marriage will help both Seekers and Followers tough out the rough patches of their own marriages far more than will the false pretense that perfect marriages are possible. There is a reason why fairy tales end with, "and they lived happily ever after." No one knows how to portray: "happily ever after." When we approach the challenges of the Christian journey together, as traveling companions, we can see the ways in which we might meet the challenges. If, on the other hand, it seems that the leaders on this journey are living more idealistic lives than most Followers and Seekers, it becomes all too easy for Seekers to give up any hope of living a better life. When listeners experience a preacher who seems to have achieved perfection, listeners can easily dismiss the message as impractical and unachievable. In contrast, listeners who hear that the preacher knows the Christian journey's difficult challenges recognize a leader who can empathize with their struggles. Followers and Seekers alike are then better able to see the likelihood of traveling the Christian path. The Christian path can be followed more securely and confidently on a regular basis when Seekers know that Followers struggle with similar difficulties on the same path.

Honesty, of course, needs to be tempered for the preacher who is tempted to pour out a sad life story or a long list of sins and temptations. Few parishioners would want to hear Jimmy Swaggart's confession of marital infidelity on a weekly basis. The preaching moment is not the time for intimate confessions, nor is it an arena for the preacher to receive a corporate group therapy session. There are ways of being appropriately honest while also allowing enough freedom of thought for persons to fill in their own stories and struggles as they listen to the message. In this reciprocal way, the message time becomes both descriptive and prescriptive. Listeners are invited to hear the biblical story, reflect on another person's experience, relate that experience to their own experience, and develop plans for improving their future.

Invitation and Inspiration

In the art of preaching, it is important to remember that there are many more listeners than preachers. Many of those listeners have important ideas and helpful insights into the same passage or theme the preacher is addressing. Regardless of theological training or divine calling, preachers are human beings and are thus limited in knowing everything that God might have intended for us to know. When speaking with Seekers, it is particularly helpful to keep this fact in mind and illustrate it in our preaching style.

Remembering this, a preacher has the power to either invite Seekers into, or exclude Seekers from, the message. Inviting Seekers into the message may be done in ways that are highly participatory, but it need not be so. It is also possible to invite

Seekers into the message in the more traditional approach of the preacher speaking while worshippers listen. For instance, the preacher can add phrases such as "I'm not certain what you think, but I've been thinking. . . ." Or, "have you ever wondered about . . . " In a Seeker-friendly sermon or message, the preacher conveys a sincere interest in asking the question, "What do *you* think?" This question will take on even more power when the preacher asks similar questions to listeners' comments following the service. Rather than simply saying "thank you" when a Seeker or Follower says, "that sermon was exactly what I needed to hear," the preacher can push the comment. "I'm glad to hear that. . . . What seemed to touch you so deeply today?" Or, "Thank you, I'd be interested to hear more about that. Would you like to have coffee this week?"

In preparing and presenting messages that are invitational in nature, the preacher will find that the messages become inspirational in an approachable way for Seekers. There is something powerful about realizing that a speaker values the opinions of listeners and that a speaker learns from his or her listeners. Often the most powerful sermon illustrations are those that come from comments worshippers have made following worship, or questions and insights Seekers and Followers have shared with a preacher. In utilizing this style of invitation, the preacher models the understanding that Followers and Seekers are indeed on a common spiritual journey. For Seekers, this can be an inspirational moment of relating to Christ and the Church in ways that the Seeker may never have thought possible.

Where We Preach

So much of preaching and worship leadership has been associated with altars, lecterns, and pulpits that it can be hard to imagine preaching from any other space. For many Seekers, however, chancel furniture is simply one more factor that distances Followers from Seekers. Pulpits can sometimes take away the warmth that so many preachers seem to have in informal settings. Often, the most effective place to offer the message is from the floor level, perhaps seated on a tall stool in the center, with notes on notecards or a music stand. Even in traditional services, when the preacher moves to the center, floor level, I can hear the invitation, "Join me on the journey." This is the message that Seekers need to hear, and that message can be strongly conveyed through proximity to the preacher.

Recently, I was visiting with a young man at the request of his parents. Having been raised in the church, he knows the traditional worship setting well. Although he and I grew very close during the time we spent together, he never attended any worship services that I led in his parents' church. One day, I asked him if he might like to come along some time. His response was fascinating. He did not complain about slow music or boring sermons. He did not whine about uncomfortable pews or early mornings. He simply asked me how a worship experience could focus on one person standing in a podium telling other people what the Bible means or how to live their lives. I admitted to him that, indeed, it did not seem appropriate to me. But for many preachers, that is exactly the style of worship their churches expect.

Even for a preacher who consciously tries to utilize an invitational and non-judgmental style, my location in the pulpit made it impossible for this young man to listen for the message. He could not see past the stereotype of preachers and sermons that he had grown up with. The following week, I preached from the floor . . . to very little complaint!

How the Message Is Conveyed

By the mid-twentieth century, Protestant worship tended to rely upon increasingly long sermons with little enhancement of the message from other media. An occasional choral anthem or hymn selection might complement the sermon. Most of the time, however, the sermon stood alone as a separate event from much of the remaining worship service.

For Seekers, the separation of sermon or message time from the other events in worship is contradictory to a worshipful experience. The Seeker is not likely to tolerate such confusion and disarray on a weekly basis. Many Followers are equally intolerant! Thus, message time with Seekers and Followers needs to encompass more than the act of preaching. As with the entire worship service, the message should flow as a part of the total worship experience.

For this reason, sermons for Seekers are often best-conveyed when they are surrounded by a drama or video that conveys the main thesis of the message. Other art forms such as dance, visual displays, slide shows, poetry, or story-telling may be utilized in the message time itself or during other times in the worship service. The use of multimedia resources will become increasingly important for Seekers of younger generations over the next 20 years. Thus, the preacher who wishes to reach these Seekers would do well to begin incorporating a diversity of resources as soon as possible.

Additionally, the use of diverse resources reflects the reality that each person learns differently. In a worship setting, where anywhere from 50 to 5000 people may be present, a traditional 30-minute lecture on the meaning of salvation is not likely to reach all of those listeners. However, a 15-minute sermon about Christ's gift on the cross, accompanied by a 10-minute drama and several songs on the same theme, is very likely to convey the uplifting message of Christian salvation.

Does this mean that worship teams have to create a new drama every week? By no means! For Seekers, variety from week to week is a good thing, as it is for many Followers. Some weeks, a drama may enhance the message. Other weeks, a vocal solo or improvisatory dance may be the most effective means of elaborating on the theme. At another time, a children's story or a movie clip may provide the most helpful illustration to convey the message. In any case, message time can be extended to include more than the words of one single preacher. When designing worship for Seekers, message time can be as diverse and creative as the worship planners allow! The crucial point is for each aspect, no matter how creative or how traditional, to be related to, or an enhancement of, the message theme for the day.

Preaching the Word

For the sermon to convey the traveling companion aspect of ministry with Seekers, many preachers will want to explore various preaching styles and forms. Limiting the message delivery to one format week after week is neither necessary nor helpful when ministering with Seekers.

The Questioning Sermon

One of the most effective means of relating to Seekers is to allow them to participate in the message time. Designing a message time that allows for questions and answers is one way to do this. In the Unitarian tradition, some preachers allow a sermon feedback time following the sermon or following the worship time. This style still allows the preacher the majority of speaking time, usually requiring participants to stay longer than the scheduled worship service time in order to have input. This style usually depends on listeners entering into a verbal dialogue with the preacher and with one another. Such a dialogue in a large-group setting with Seekers may be more difficult than in a small, intimate gathering of Followers.

However, gathering questions on note cards during the service to be used in the message time can alleviate some of the difficulties that a sermon feedback format presents. For the preacher who is not comfortable with extemporaneous speaking or who needs more preparation time to respond to challenging questions, note cards could be gathered to be addressed in a future message. Although less helpful for the Seekers who are present, this method does present a "cliffhanger" that may attract Seekers to return for a second week.

If the preacher is willing and able, answering the questions in the same service can provide a profound experience of theological reflection and faith journeying for both Seekers and Followers. In order to streamline questions and plan a thematic worship service with this style of "sermon," the worship outline can include the printed scripture for the day and a brief explanation of the theme. The instructions for writing questions may even include some direction toward which the questions might be aimed. Be forewarned, however: Some questions will be unexpected!

The Seeker Service Welcomes the Stranger to Worship!
Worship Figure G

JUNE 26, 1997
11:30 a.m.

MESSAGE
"WELCOMING ANGELS UNAWARE"

For today's message, we will explore the meaning of welcoming the stranger, and of the demands placed on believer's lives by Christ's warning about the sheep and the goats. As you read this morning's scripture passage (on the other side) you are invited to note any questions you have about this passage or theme on the 3 x 5 note cards provided. Ushers will collect them during the song "Helping Hand." As many questions as possible will be answered during our message today.

SONGS AND VIDEOS

"Helping Hand"
Written & Performed by Amy Grant

"Jesu, Jesu"
Hymnal, page 432

"What If God Was One of Us?"
Written & Performed by Joan Osborne

READINGS and DRAMATIC SKETCHES
FROM THE HOLY BIBLE
Matthew 25:31–45 & Hebrews 13:1–2

FROM *RANDOM ACTS OF KINDNESS*
"Every Human Being is Your Counterpart"

SPECIAL OPPORTUNITIES
THE SACRAMENT OF HOLY COMMUNION

Sacraments are sacred moments of connection with God,
times of mystery where we are invited into God's
unconditional love in the community of faith.
Please feel free to participate by taking the bread and
juice, singing or meditating.

MATTHEW 25:31–45

"When the Son of Man comes in his glory,
and all the angels with him,
    then he will sit on the throne of his glory.
All the nations will be gathered before him, and he will separate people one from another as a shepherd
separates the sheep from the goats,
    and he will put the sheep at his right hand and the goats at the left.
Then the king will say to those at his right hand, 'Come, you that are
blessed by my Father, inherit the kingdom prepared for you from the
foundation of the world;
    for I was hungry and you gave me food,
        I was thirsty and you gave me something to drink,
            I was a stranger and you welcomed me,
    I was naked and you gave me clothing,
        I was sick and you took care of me,
            I was in prison and you visited me.'
Then the righteous will answer him,
    'Lord, when was it that we saw you hungry and gave you food,
    or thirsty and gave you something to drink?
And when was it that we saw you a stranger and welcomed you,

129

or naked and gave you clothing?
And when was it that we saw you sick or in prison and visited you?'
And the king will answer them, 'Truly I tell you, just as you did it to one of the least of
these who are members of my family, you did it to me.'

Then he will say to those at his left hand,
'You that are accursed, depart from me into the eternal fire prepared for the devil and his angels;
for I was hungry and you gave me no food,
I was thirsty and you gave me nothing to drink,
I was a stranger and you did not welcome me,
naked and you did not give me clothing,
sick and in prison and you did not visit me.'
Then they also will answer,
'Lord, when was it that we saw you hungry or thirsty or a stranger or naked or sick or in prison, and did not take care of you?'
Then he will answer them, 'Truly I tell you, just as you did not do it to one of the least of these, you did not do it to me.'

HEBREWS 13:1–2

Let mutual love continue.
Do not neglect to show hospitality to strangers,
for by doing that some have entertained angels without knowing it.[1]

Worship Figure G illustrates one of the worship programs in which this type of message is presented. The invitation to question and dialogue is offered as the central focus for the message. Participants are encouraged to read over the scriptures and theme for the day before writing their questions. Questions are collected early enough before the message time for the preacher to review the questions and gather his or her thoughts. (Note that this order of Seeker worship is not chronological, allowing for spontaneity on the part of the worship leadership.) In this case, the message is designed with the intention of closing the message time with a reading from *Random Acts of Kindness*. However, the preacher is free to go in a different direction, if the questions indicate that necessity.

Inviting people to write their names and phone numbers or addresses on the index cards provides a helpful contact with

Seekers. Seekers are then assured of receiving responses, if they wish to be contacted personally. Likewise, the evangelism team and pastor have one more contact point for reaching the Seekers who have attended worship. Additional leeway is given to the preacher when it is made clear that while some questions may not be answered today, many will then be addressed in subsequent weeks. Answering several of the questions during the current worship service addresses the needs of one-time worship attendees. Dangling the carrot that promises other questions will be addressed later encourages persons to return for future messages. In doing both, the preacher strikes a balance between the needs of the Seekers and the evangelistic goals of the Followers. The preacher also allows a certain flexibility if certain questions need further preparation before being addressed in the message time.

When preparing for the Questioning Sermon, the preacher will want to study the scripture text and related theological themes carefully and diligently. Use of traditional sermon aids such as commentaries or preaching manuals is only one aspect of such preparation. The preacher will want to observe similar themes in novels, television, movies, newspapers, and magazines. This style of sermon is in no way an easy way to reduce the amount of time required to prepare a good sermon! Likewise, the preacher will want to anticipate possible questions, perhaps through a weekly study group or through informal conversations with Seekers she or he encounters during the preparation time. Preachers who take the time to "tune in" to the issues that concern Seekers find that they are better able to anticipate the questions Seekers ask. I find that certain themes and questions arise again and again. In particular, challenging passages like Jesus' parable of the separation of the Sheep and the Goats or his command that we must forgive people 70 times 7 arouse predictable concerns and struggles for Seekers and Followers. Themes such as forgiveness, anger, judgment, God's love, human behavior, evil in the world, and human stress seem to arise often from the listeners I minister with. Becoming familiar with the concerns of the Seekers and Followers in your midst will make this preaching style more manageable and attainable. Ultimately, each preacher arrives at that stage of relationship with Seekers in his or her own time.

Finally, the preacher who presents a Questioning Sermon will not want to enter the message time without a good amount of prayer undergirding the message. Prior to studying commentaries or sermon articles, the preacher will want to spend time praying for the persons who will hear the message. Prayers for the preacher's own discernment, wisdom, and guidance is also helpful. God's guiding wisdom can help the preacher to prepare for the unexpected questions, to anticipate the common concerns, and to focus thoughts when preparing for the Questioning Sermon. The preacher's prayers throughout the sermon preparation time and the week prior to the message come to fruition during the worship service. In other words, the prayers that helped the preacher to focus often help the question and answer time to flow more smoothly. Those same prayers can help to calm the preacher's nerves when faced with difficult or unexpected consequences. In addition, Followers can be enlisted in a weekly prayer ministry to ask God to help the preacher discern the movement of the Holy Spirit during the message time. Seekers can even be invited to offer their own prayers in the worship service to help create an atmosphere of openness and receptivity to the leading of the Holy Spirit during worship.

Preaching the "Questioning Sermon" is a wonderful invitation into the Christian journey for Seekers. It is also a broadening exercise for the preacher, and a challenging experience for Followers. Although not an easy or comfortable task for most preachers, this sermon format will bring growth on the Christian journey that may never have occurred otherwise!

The Story Sermon

When preaching to Seekers, preachers need to remember that most Seekers do not know the biblical story. Even many

Followers yearn for a more thorough understanding of their Judeo-Christian heritage! Yet, traditional preaching often assumes that Sunday School teachers and Bible study leaders will fill in the gaps. Such assumptions are dangerous. The reality is that an alarmingly large number of Seekers and Followers fill in these gaps by watching Hollywood movies or by reading historical novels. Preachers who are interested in how biblical characters and stories are perceived will want to take the time to tell the stories themselves. In doing so, we do more than simply introducing the biblical stories to Seekers. We also invite Seekers and Followers to engage the biblical story and relate it to contemporary life.

Re-telling the biblical story or preaching the "Story Sermon" can be a powerful and effective way of reaching Seekers with the message time in worship. For example, the story of Jesus' Passion (Trial and Death) is central to the Christian message. Yet, this story is often lost through the celebratory nature of Palm Sunday, formerly called Passion Sunday. However, the Passion Play tradition of Europe illustrates how effectively the Story Sermon can reach people from all walks of life. Even in modern times, Followers and Seekers plan European vacations around the scheduled portrayal of this ancient play at Oberammergau each year. Many of the Seekers who attend this event return home to begin visiting church, perhaps for the first time in their lives.

When re-telling the biblical story, consider dramatic options such as portraying a character within the story. This character can then share the scripture event and possible meanings of the event from the character's perspective. For instance, Peter could re-tell the story of denying Jesus three times and then reflect on what impact that had on his own life and ministry as a disciple. Appendix A offers an example of re-telling the story of the woman with the issue of blood. In this narrative sermon, the woman not only tells her story, but reflects on theological themes and personal growth that came from her encounter with Jesus.

133

Of course, when a drama group or willing actors are available, it can be wonderful to have a full-scale re-enactment of one of Jesus' miracles or parables. A simple re-enactment can be achieved with the use of "reader's theater." In this setting, the characters simply read their lines, thus re-telling the biblical story in a very personal way, without utilizing actions or movement. For instance, Esther and Mordecai can re-tell the story of Haman's persecution of the Jewish people and Esther's intervention on behalf of her people.

When preaching a Story Sermon, most preachers will want to leave the pulpit. The simple act of leaving the pulpit invites people into the story and creates a warmer story-telling atmosphere. When the preacher both tells the story and relates how the story has has impacted his or her life and ministry, listeners are shown a way of relating the story to their own lives. This can be one of the most powerful methods of preaching the Story Sermon. During one particularly meaningful Good Friday service, three preachers shared their own experiences of what Jesus' death on the cross had meant in their lives. In so doing, they re-told the Good Friday story of Jesus' trial and death in a compelling way.

Another possibility for the Story Sermon utilizes fictional stories to illustrate a biblical message or story. Likewise, parables can be re-worked using modern images and occurrences to bring home the relevance of Jesus' teachings to contemporary life.

By telling stories, we are truly being Jesus' disciples, for Jesus taught some of his most profound messages through the art of story-telling. Jesus relied upon story-telling, particularly when he was preaching to Seekers and to Followers who had lost sight of the journey. In Jesus' stories, he was careful to utilize common images, daily experiences, and believable characters. He also left the stories to speak for themselves, an important lesson for preachers who are used to drawing conclusions at the end of any message.

In any event, the simple act of story-telling is a marvelous way to connect with Seekers. A good story, told well and spoken with a genuine passion, will capture listeners in a way that traditional sermons seldom can. For the preacher who wants to learn more about the art of story-telling, written resources and workshops are readily available.

The Meditational Sermon

For worship planners who are designing worship experiences of a reflective or meditative nature, traditional sermons may need to be replaced by centering time and meditative reflections. Again, written resources and workshops on leading guided meditation are abundantly available for the preacher who wants to learn more about this style of spiritual leadership.

In the Meditation Sermon, the preacher strives to become unimportant in the worship experience. In this way, the Seeker is invited to connect directly with God and listen for God's message as it comes to worshippers during the time of meditation or reflection. Although this is most often achieved in a guided meditation setting, there are other possibilities for offering a Meditation Sermon. The preacher may choose to read a scripture along with some creative writings, reflective thoughts, or poems related to that scripture. Likewise, instrumental or vocal music could be intertwined with the scripture readings to further assist in the reflection process.

The Taize' style of worshipping, through repetitive congregational music and scripture, can also be a very effective method of inviting Seekers into a comfortable Meditative worship experience. Although a sermon or message may not even be offered in this setting, the worship leader or cantor serves in a priestly role. Recognizing this priestly presence helps the leader to be effective in connecting Seekers and Followers with the Holy.

The challenge in offering a Meditation Sermon is to overcome our stereotypes about the responsibility for preachers to "preach the Word." Since the Reformation, this has come to mean the responsibility to exegete and explain certain scripture passages in every worship service. In the effective Meditation

Sermon, the preacher gives up that stereotype by recognizing that God is readily found through ritual, music, liturgy, and silence.

Silence is perhaps the most important key to any meditative service, and the Meditation Sermon is specifically designed to allow for that time of silence in the message time. Naming that time of silence a "Time of Reflection" helps worship participants to understand the focus of such silent time. The popularity of Taize' services and many New Age styles of worship certainly point to the human yearning for times of meditation and reflection. Worship planners need not, however, become experts in alternative styles of worship to offer a meditative mood. Even a traditional Christian worship service can be designed to promote the meditative experience. Worship Figure H offers an example of a Christian worship experience that incorporates a Native American style of centering. Although the words for the centering time and blessing would not normally be printed in a worship program, they are provided here for worship planners. This may help planners to imagine a centering process in this style of worship. Many Seekers will be very appreciative of meditative opportunities of this kind.

A TIME OF REFLECTION AND WORSHIP
Worship Figure H

Welcome!

Today, we begin the season of Advent, a 4-week season of reflection and meditation as we prepare for the celebration of Jesus' birth on Christmas. During this season, we are encouraged to reflect on the past year and where we have experienced both God's presence and absence. We are invited to prepare for a new year of walking with God, and to celebrate the gift of God's unconditional love symbolized in the birth of God's Son, Jesus the Christ.

MUSIC FOR MEDITATION AND FELLOWSHIP
Shadowfax   "One Winter Morning"

OPENING THOUGHTS

A TIME FOR CENTERING (All are invited to stand
and face the directions.)

Paul reminds us that Christ is the center of creation,
   of our lives, and of the world.
We seek the wisdom of directions.
From each direction we return to the center
   reminded that Christ brings healing and salvation
     and by God's Spirit renews the face of the earth.
Let us be silent as we face our center point.

Let us face East. (All persons face East.)
From the East, the direction of the rising sun,
   we glean wisdom and knowledge
     through desert silences and humble service.
Enable us, O God, to be wise in our actions
   and in our use of the resources of the earth,
     sharing them in justice, partaking of them in gratitude.
From the wisdom of the East, we return to Christ our Center.
(All persons return facing Center)

Let us face South.(All persons face South.)
From the South come guidance and the beginning and end of life.
May we walk good paths, O God,
   living on the earth as sisters and brothers should,
   rejoicing in one another's blessing,
   sympathizing in one another's sorrows,
   and together look to you, seeking the new heaven and earth.
From the guidance of the South, we return to Christ our Center.
(All persons return facing Center.)

Let us face West. (All persons face West.)
From the West come purifying waters.
We pray that water might be pure and available to all,
   and that we, too, may be purified
so that life may be sustained and nurtured
   over the entire face of the earth.
From the healing of the West, we return to Christ our Center.
(All persons return facing Center.)

Let us face North. (All persons face North.)
From the North come strong winds and gentle breezes.
May the air we breathe be purified
and may our lives feel that breath of the Spirit,
   strengthening and encouraging us.
From the refreshing breezes of the North, we return to Christ our
   Center.
(All persons return facing Center.)

137

If we walked a path in each direction, the sacred paths would form a cross.
Returning to the center, we discover Christ,
    who calls us and challenges us.
(TRADITIONAL LAKOTA TRIBE PRAYER, ALT.)[2]

SONG OF CENTERING (standing)   "Shawnee Traveling Song"
    Hey a loma, Hey a loma. Hey o-pa-la-ma.
    Hey opaloma, Hey o-pa-lay

READINGS OF THE SEASON
Chapter 33, Verses 14–16 from the
Book of Jeremiah in The Holy Bible
The 25th Song or Psalm in The Holy Bible

VIDEO   "Tell Me All Your Thoughts On God"   Dishwalla

REFLECTING TOGETHER   "Repairing and Preparing"

A READING   from "Simple Abundance" by Sarah Ban Breathnach

CLOSING WORDS
May the blessing of God, fountain of living water,
    flow within us as a river of life.
May we drink deep of her wisdom.
May we never thirst again.
May we go through life refreshing many as a sign of healing for all;
    through the One who is Life eternal. Amen.

The Exegetical Sermon

For those preachers whose style leans toward the traditional, a few basic adaptations can help any style of preaching connect with Seekers. The sermon or message should be genuine and important to the preacher. If the preacher is uninterested in the message, there is an excellent chance no one else will be interested either. Moreover, the sermon should not appear "canned" or formulaic. If listeners are expected to follow scripture during the message time, scriptures can be printed on handouts each week for the worshippers. Likewise, if listeners are expected to remember five specific points of the message, providing a sermon outline or a space in the program for notes (along with pencils or pens) can be very helpful.

If the preacher's style includes the use of traditional theological or doctrinal terms, each term will need to be defined during its usage in the message. Again, notes provided with the worship program can be very helpful for providing this "glossary" to Seekers. Likewise, if the preacher quotes important theologians or church leaders, those persons will need to be "defined" when they are mentioned. For instance, when quoting John Wesley, the United Methodist preacher might say, "John Wesley, the founder of Methodism, has taught us these things."

Whatever the preaching style, the practical application of the message to the Christian life is a helpful connection point for both Seekers and Followers alike. More importantly than any specific preaching style however, the preacher's attitude of open acceptance and invitational approach will reach Seekers effectively. The warmth and love expressed in a non-judgmental and invitational sermon—no matter how challenging that message may be—welcomes Seekers onto the spiritual journey in a way that few can ignore.

As with almost every aspect of reaching Seekers that we have explored thus far, the personal connection remains the single most important element of ministering with Seekers. The preacher who exudes warmth, offers sincerity, and displays genuine faith and love will reach Seekers with almost any preaching format. This said, however, some formats remain more helpful than others in helping Seekers to deepen their faith. This goal of deepening faith and pursuing the spiritual journey makes it worthwhile for preachers to explore new means of communicating. In all of our outreach efforts, we are called to offer the good news to people of all the nations. In order to help Seekers become Followers, preachers will want to find ways of communicating that Seekers can accept. As preachers do so, the Holy Spirit will be better able to work in the lives of both Seekers and Followers as people of faith grow together.

Notes

1. Scripture Readings taken from the New Revised Standard Version of the Holy Bible.

2. All printed resources in this service are used, with permission, from *The United Methodist Book of Worship*.

CHAPTER SIX

Go Ye into All the World

As you have probably guessed by now, planning worship for Seekers is not a ministry for the faint of heart. Nor is it a ministry for lone rangers or sole entrepreneurs. When Followers begin connecting with Seekers, Followers quickly discover that there are many things to learn and many opportunities for failure. Church leaders who try to go it alone will find the level of frustration high and the rate of success low. However, Followers who recognize the challenge of connecting with Seekers also recognize that a team of Followers is better able to connect with Seekers than is a single leader.

Planning worship for Seekers provides an exciting opportunity for pastors to utilize church staff members and volunteers as a team when planning worship. Worship committees that formerly have been relegated to ordering candles and training acolytes can now be given responsibility for organizing advertising campaigns and recruiting artists from the community outside of the church. Church musicians who have long petitioned for more voice in music selection can now be encouraged to research new music for reaching Seekers. Preparing music in an integrated worship team can become a fulfilling part of the musician's ministry. Pastors, who have long thought that worship was a responsibility only for the ordained, will quickly learn that sharing worship responsibility adds excitement and enjoyment, not only to the worship planning process, but to the worship experience itself.

Before a church or worship team embarks on this new adventure, however, it is crucial for the congregation and church leaders to spend a great deal of time in prayer and planning. Long before the first public worship service, prayerful support and careful planning will be needed to discern and design the most effective ministry possible with Seekers. Church leaders who can discern the gifts that they and the congregation possess will be better able to design worship and Seeker ministries that incorporate those talents. Everyone benefits when a new ministry builds on the church's strengths, rather than its weaknesses!

Worship Planning Teams will also want to become familiar with what other churches and worship leaders are doing to reach Seekers, both locally and nationally. Time spent here will help your worship team target the specific group of Seekers with whom your church is called to minister. This can also be a valuable step in producing the most effective ministry possible. Churches that are already reaching Seekers have learned from their mistakes and are usually willing to share what they have learned along the way. Churches that are advertising to Seekers, but are not reaching them, also have valuable lessons to share. Ministries that fail to reach Seekers have as much to teach churches as those ministries that succeed in reaching Seekers. Learning from others' mistakes and successes will enhance your new ministries with Seekers while also offering many new and creative ideas your worship Planning Team may wish to borrow.

During this initial planning and dreaming process, your team will also need to evaluate the church's readiness for this new ministry. If a church is not prepared to include Seekers in each of its program and ministry areas, it is probably not ready to accept Seekers into full Christian fellowship. This needs to be considered prayerfully by any team that wants to reach Seekers with a specific worship service or ministry. Seekers who respond to a particular ministry immediately sense if they are being excluded from other program and ministry opportunities

142

in the church. Seekers cannot be expected to stay in the church, or experience the full realm of Christian spirituality, if they are denied full participation. Thus, a church that wants to begin a new ministry with Seekers is best prepared if it recognizes and rejoices that Seekers may begin to connect with several of the church's ministries.

If the team is planning for its Seeker worship to be an additional worship service, several steps need to be taken before the process moves too far along. First, the team will need to lay the necessary groundwork to support this new mission of the church by recruiting leadership from within the congregation, advertising the event before it happens, and by setting goals. As the new venture is planned, the pastor and Planning Team need to be cautioned against the temptation to ignore the current worshipping congregation. In the excitement of initiating a new ministry, planners easily fall into the trap of paying too little attention to already existing ministries. Moreover, pastors and leaders who are invested in a successful start to the new ministry may unintentionally set up a competition between currently existing worship services and the new one being added. This is particularly seductive if some of the current church leaders have opposed the new ministry. Such temptations must be faced and overcome if your ministry with Seekers is to become an integrated part of the entire church's ministry. Such integration is essential for the benefit of both Seekers and Followers. After all, the Christian journey is something for Seekers to join, not something they need to start alone. The church's greatest gifts to Seekers are the gifts of community and a faith journey shared with new-found friends.

Choosing and Establishing the Ministry Team

Because this ministry team is embarking on a new and long-term ministry, team members need to be chosen carefully. Members should believe in team ministry. This is no ministry for those who work best in isolation, nor is it a ministry that pastors can accomplish alone. Additionally, contemporary expressions of worship are foreign to many pastors, and increasing the number of planners will expand the diversity and creativity of ideas—important elements of Seeker worship! The original team for this ministry may need to be an investigation team (see below). This provides the opportunity for team members to bow out gracefully should the investigation take this new worship ministry in directions unlike that originally envisioned. It will also allow the original team to involve some people with marketing or demographic specialties who do not need to be a part of the ongoing worship Planning Team.

However, the team will need to represent a wide diversity of talents and interests from the beginning. Many Worship Planning Teams make the mistake of involving a large pool of creative talent with little thought to the need for organizers and administrators. Other worship teams are full of detail-oriented people but lack visionaries. The strongest team includes many players. A strong team needs dreamers and visionaries who can see the big picture and push the team into the future at every turn. A strong team also includes a good number of creative and artistic persons. These artists provide ideas and insights for creating worship that is both innovative and appealing to Seekers. The team will need a self-confident leader who can integrate the many creative ideas and exciting visions of the team into a realistic plan of action. And the leader will need team members who can serve as managers, administrators, and organizers to implement the plan as it moves forward. Although workers need not be members of the initial team, workers will be needed to support the team and do the work of this ministry. Workers with the spiritual gift of service are ideal in bringing the plan to fruition, but the workers need not sit in on every planning meeting. After all, their hands will be full when the work begins!

Every team member needs to sense a calling to this ministry. Yet, this sense of calling seldom occurs before the team members are introduced to Seekers and to the need for worship and ministry with Seekers in mind. Thus, it is often best if the initial invitation onto the team is an invitation onto an Investigating Team that explores the possibilities for this new ministry. After the investigation stage, team leaders can discern which team members have developed a passion and interest for this ministry. Such passion and interest are often a sign of God's calling. Team members who enter into this ministry just to try something new or to gain an arena for promoting their own talents will not effectively minister with Seekers. Rather, such team members can destroy the ministry by eroding the original intention of developing a Seeker-friendly worship service. However, team members who develop this passion for Seekers and discern God's call to reach Seekers during the investigation process will become invaluable leaders in the new worship planning process.

Many of the people mentioned as "Tools" in the previous chapter are ideal members of a Seeker Worship Planning Team. Planning Team members may include musicians, artists, organizers, writers, and pastors. All members of the worship Planning Team will meet regularly during the investigation stage. Those who plan to continue on the team will continue to meet after the investigation stage, often monthly. Although well-established teams may choose to meet seasonally or bi-annually, planning meetings will be common, necessary, and frequent in the initial stages of new worship planning.

Such a team should consist of more persons than the "typical" church committee. Incorporating not only creative people and strong leaders from within the church, but also creative people and community leaders from outside the church, will greatly enhance the effectiveness of a Seeker Worship Planning Team. As such, the team already begins to represent the diversity that the worship service is designed to attract.

145

STAGES OF NEW SEEKER WORSHIP MINISTRY

STAGE	TEAMS NEEDED	TIME FRAME
1. Investigating	Investigating Team	3–6 months
2. Initial Planning	Worship Planning Team Marketing Team	3–6 months
3. Worship Planning	Worship Planning Team	3 months before first service; thereafter, ongoing preparation of services approx. 3 months in advance
	(Marketing Team does ongoing work)	
4. Incorporating	Nurturing/Integration Team	Ongoing

Checking It Out: Investigating Ministry Needs

As the initial team comes together, team members can discuss their instincts and interests regarding the need for Seeker ministry in their community. From these instincts, the Investigating Team can then explore demographic information to begin narrowing the possible ministry options. Social service and local government information can help the team discern what the actual ministry needs might be in the community. Finally, the Investigating Team will want to do some field work, where team members search for Seekers to discuss ministry possibilities with them. As the Investigating Team gathers this information, the team can then begin to develop a plan for the new worship service or new ministry.

At this point, it is critical that the Investigating Team accurately gauge what reaction the local congregation might have to this new ministry. Followers who are active in church leadership, as well as Followers who are less active, can be interviewed or invited into informal small group discussions for this investigation. In order to prepare for objections to the new ministry proposal, team members will want to note concerns that Followers bring to these discussions. Team members may also find potential workers and additional team members from these discussions. Additionally, team members may want to discuss the new ministry possibilities with church leaders and pastors from other communities of faith. Besides bringing new ideas for your ministry to light, this will help team members anticipate potential problems in the ecumenical or Interfaith community. Conversations with Followers in other communities of faith can also initiate a collegiality of common concern for Seekers. Other communities of faith may wish to help Seekers find their way into a church home where Seekers are intentionally welcomed into a worship experience or ministry opportunity.

Although the Investigation Team need not wear out team members by dragging the investigation stage to unnecessary lengths, thorough inquiries early in the process will prevent many problems and failures from developing later in the process. This stage can provide a wonderful opportunity to educate people about Seekers and Seekers' spiritual needs. At the same time, team members will be building a coalition of support for this new ministry within the community.

Getting Ready: Initial Planning Processes

As the Investigating Team gathers data, team members will begin to discern what format this worship service or ministry is likely to take. At this point, additional planners may need to be incorporated into the team. Some investigators may choose to leave the team and explore other ministries. As the Initial Planning Team is formed, it is critical that the team share openly the material and data gathered during the investigation stage. With data in hand, the Planning Team can outline its Concept Development Proposal for this new ministry. If the team wishes to incorporate ideas from the church's larger leadership team, a basic framework can be outlined or several alternatives can be listed. In either case, the proposal or the framework will need to be taken to a larger group of Followers within the church (probably the formal church leadership) in order to gain widespread support for the new worship service or ministry.

Rallying the Troops: Selling the New Ministry

In order to promote new ministries to the current church leadership, pastors and leaders must often package and sell the ministry. Although it is sometimes easier in the short-run to bully the current leadership team and speed the process along, that process typically results in a short-lived ministry. For Seekers, the new worship service and any other ministries specifically designed for the integration of Seekers need to be long-lasting and firmly established. Thus, an Integration or Nurturing Team will need to be established alongside the Worship Planning Team in order to plan for the integration of Seekers into the community of faith. Seekers are not likely to be "fast recruits," nor are they likely to grow quickly in their faith journeys. Ministries that welcome Seekers need to survive for many years. Time is necessary for Seekers to slowly investigate the community, enter the community step by step, and grow spiritually to the point where Seekers become Followers and evangelists to other Seekers.

Elements of a Concept Development Proposal[1]

WHO
> Who will do the work? Who will oversee?
> To whom will the outreach (worship service) be offered?

WHAT
> What outreach will be offered?
> What type of worship experience will be offered?

WHY
> Why do this ministry?
> What ministry need does this answer?

WHEN
> What is the planning time line?
> When will the ministry begin?
> How long will the ministry continue?
> When will evaluation occur?

WHERE
> Where will the ministry be hosted?
> Where will the ministry recipients come from?

COST
> How many people (paid & volunteer) will be needed to staff this ministry?
> How much time and money will it take to provide this ministry?

IMPLICATIONS
> What will the impact be . . .
> To the ministry recipients?
> To the ministers involved?
> To other Followers in the church?
> To other ministries in the church?

CONSEQUENCES
> What are the expected consequences?
> What might the unanticipated consequences be?

In "selling" the idea of Seeker ministry to your current church leadership, you and your team leaders can share the research and knowledge that has convinced you of the importance of Seeker worship and ministry. Ideally, this research and knowledge will be shared during the initial investigation stage of the new ministry. After all, inviting church leaders into the journey of understanding and appreciating Seekers is good training for inviting Seekers onto the Christian journey of faith!

The leadership of the church will also need to feel the pastor's and the Planning Team's passion for this new ministry. Shying away from one's calling is seldom effective in persuading others to support such a calling—particularly when the calling is one as bold as creating worship for reaching Seekers! Testimonies from Seekers-turned-Followers can also be very effective in reaching the hearts and minds of church leaders who may initially be resistant. In both cases, the church leadership will need to hear a clearly-articulated mission and vision for the ministry. If the pastor and worship Planning Team already have definite plans in mind, then the Concept Development Proposal should be carefully outlined and fully presented to the church leadership at this point. Otherwise, the proposal will need to be developed immediately following church leadership approval.

Take heart. Almost every Follower in this day and age has at least one beloved family member or friend who is a Seeker. Inviting Followers to share stories of those persons in their lives with one another will often provide some of the most powerful testimonies to the importance of designing worship and ministry with Seekers in mind. This can be particularly effective when the Investigation or Planning Team invites resistant church leaders to name Seekers who are important in their lives. Dr. Stanley Menking, demographic and church growth consultant, persuades many curmudgeons to initiate ministries with Generation X Seekers simply by asking them to name the unchurched Generation X people in their family. When the vague term "Seeker" is given a face and a name, Christian leaders usually feel the necessity of reaching Seekers.

Ready to Roar: the Planning Process

As the Worship Planning Team begins to design worship services to reach Seekers, the team will face many choices. Before the process moves too far forward, however, several decisions must be made.

Whom Will We Reach?

Every time I present this question to a local church, I meet resistance. Since the Body of Christ includes all people, regardless of gender, race, or class, many churches feel uncomfortable trying to target only one group of people. Although scripture is clear that the Church is not meant to exclude anyone, scripture is equally clear that local faith communities (local churches) have always tended to reach specific groups within that community. The truth is, the church who tries to reach everyone most often reaches no one. One of the beautiful aspects of reaching Seekers from the younger generations is that much of the church's desire for diversity will take care of itself the minute that Followers invite Seekers onto the journey. In spite of the protests that I hear from local churches, I see the least amount of diversity amongst Followers. The greatest amount of diversity is often found amongst Seekers—even Seekers of a single demographic group—who are looking for ways to enter into a Christian community's faith journey.

Indeed, the wise church leader will help the Planning Team focus on a specific group of Seekers in the community surrounding the church. In order for the Planning Team to determine the group to be reached, prayer and discernment are essential. The Planning Team will want to incorporate as many research methods as possible to reach these decisions, particularly if an Investigating Team was not used beforehand. Local demographic information can be combined with personal interviews with Seekers. The Planning Team's participation in community events and acquaintance with entertainment establishments frequented by Seekers can also help in the information-gathering or investigation stage.

As information is gathered, the team will want to decide what faith traditions and cultural traditions this new ministry can offer to Seekers. An honest appraisal of the local church's traditions will help to determine which Seekers are likely to receive effective ministry from your local church. The team will also want to discuss what faith backgrounds and theological understandings these Seekers may bring with them to your church. This will also help to focus the new Seeker ministry. Finally, the Planning Team will want to consider whether a specific age group or social group of Seekers would be most effectively reached by this ministry. For instance, each Wednesday night, St. Luke's United Methodist Church in Houston offers an alternative worship experience that focuses on outreach to single and divorced persons who are in need of healing and reflection time. Because of the specific design of that worship service, Seekers and Followers come to worship with the knowledge that their needs for lament, grief, and healing will be addressed. Such clarity can assure Seekers that the worship experience will meet their needs. Such clarity will also help some Seekers to realize that looking elsewhere for a worship experience may better serve their interests.

What We Can Offer

After determining (or estimating) the group of Seekers to whom this new worship service will be aimed, the team will be better able to design the appropriate type of worship experience. A review of Chapter 3 will be very helpful to the team at this point. The new service may be a traditional type of worship with an intentional Seeker-friendly atmosphere. Or, the team may determine that the church would do best to adapt its current traditional worship experience to become more Seeker-friendly over a period of time.

The new service may be an adaptation of a praise and celebration service, again transformed into a Seeker-friendly experience. Or, the team may determine that certain aspects of a praise-style of worship can be combined with a Traditional or Seeker-style service to offer the best alternative worship for a given group of Seekers.

The team may decide that the Seekers to whom this church is called to serve will need a total Seeker experience. In this case, the team will want to determine which style of Seeker Service is most appropriate: the Anti-Church Seeker Service, the Sunday Schooled Seeker Service, or the Unchurched Seeker Service. Again, the team may want to consider a blending of styles and approaches to broaden the potential group of Seekers to be reached.

Particularly when the team is looking at a new worship service or a drastically different worship service than one currently being offered, the team will want to consider financial needs. The cost of adding multi-media equipment can be quite high, but can often be funded by individual donors who see the need for this ministry. Some religious denominations even provide grant funding for this type of financial need. If the team is considering alternate locations, the cost of rental space or interior improvements to the space will need to be calculated. If additional paid staff will be hired for this new ministry, funding for those staff persons should be raised prior to the worship service's implementation. The assumption that such funding will be generated from the new service is a recipe for failure.

As the team looks at how much it is willing to spend on this new ministry with Seekers, one very crucial fact must be faced. Seeker ministry is not likely to become self-funding for quite some time. You can expect it to take at least three to five years before this ministry is self-supporting. Certainly, in three to five years, the team will be able to determine whether or not it is successfully reaching Seekers. But such a determination will be determined by things like worship attendance, Christian commitments, and involvement levels in ministry by Seekers. Remember, evaluating the success of your ministry with Seekers should not focus too heavily on their financial commitment to the church in the early stages. This said, however, within a 10-year time frame, the ministry should easily be self-supporting and solidly funded. Nevertheless, creating a new ministry with the intention of the ministry becoming "self-supporting" is hardly a goal in keeping with the Christian concept of building a mutually supportive Body of Christ. Thus, I never advise churches to separate new ministry costs if such a separation will lead to a continual temptation of thinking "us versus them" or "self versus other." Such identification is a great hindrance in reaching Seekers for Christ!

As the team considers its various options, keep in mind what impact the influx of Seekers will have on your local church. The church will need to be prepared to offer more than just a one-hour worship experience. Thus, Followers throughout the church will need to be educated about relating to Seekers. Followers can be invited into a variety of hospitality ministries related to the worship service itself. Greeters and ushers will be needed, as will host Followers to attend the refreshment and friendship time following worship each week. If a telephone and advertising campaign is planned to kick off the first service, phone callers and letter-writers will also be needed. Most importantly, Followers who lead Bible studies, who assist with visitation and pastoral care, or who organize social activities for the church, will need to be trained and prepared to greet Seekers. For, as Seekers become more integrated into the life of your church, they will become interested in these ministry areas. If Seekers are not invited into these ministry areas, they may become frustrated and seek out a church where they are welcome. Here, it is helpful if an Integrating or Nurturing Team is formed to plan and facilitate the welcoming and nurturing of Seekers into the midst of

Followers. Such a team can be instrumental in helping a Seeker ministry or Seeker worship service become a part of the whole church. If a careful effort is not expended toward integrating Seekers into the total life of the church, Seekers will most likely remain isolated from the body of Followers.

All of these aspects of ministry with Seekers are important if the worship service for Seekers is to have a long-term impact on the life and growth of Seekers and Followers in the church. Thinking through the various dimensions of this new ministry will help churches to see how very much that they have to offer Seekers, not just today but tomorrow as well.

Planning the Worship Services

After the Planning Team has completed the investigation process and determined which style of Seeker worship to offer, the planning work must begin. At this point, the pastor and team leaders will need to re-assess the composition of the team. Some team members will need to use their talents elsewhere; others will want to use their talents elsewhere. Some team members will want to change roles within the team; others will want to increase their involvement on the team as the team enters this new stage. Also, new team members may want to join the planning process at this point.

After the team has been re-formed, it will need to appoint a Planning Leader. This person is most often a good organizer who will oversee the process of implementation. Often, this leader is most effective if she or he works well with both artists and administrators. Because of the enormous amount of talent and strong investment in ideas, conflict resolution will be a normal part of almost any team management role!

Before the team begins, the pastor(s) on the team will need a rough idea of the time required for planning music and other arts. Each pianist or song leader can communicate to the pastor the average length of time needed to pick or compose new songs, order or arrange the music or songbooks, obtain copyright permissions, and rehearse the songs prior to Sunday morning. Each drama coordinator can decide the length of time needed to write or find a vignette to illustrate the scripture or sermon topic. Finally, the musicians and artists can communicate their visions for music and art ministry to the pastor(s) .

Pastors, likewise, need to inform musicians of their planning needs. The preacher's process of sermon preparation may need to be adapted to the new planning process; or the planning process may be designed around the preacher's preparation style. The team may want to establish cues to alert the musicians that light background music is needed during an unexpected situation in worship. Or, cues may need to be shared with the pastor when a technical difficulty makes a certain plan impossible to implement during the service.

The team can also determine what expectations are required of each worship leader during the service. For instance, team members should discuss whether they will listen attentively to the sermon, smile during the opening songs, talk informally with one another as a part of worship leadership, and stand or kneel during the prayer. Worship leaders will eventually begin to work more synergistically, but most of the worship flow will need to be carefully planned and detailed during the initial worship services. Likewise, team members will determine what responsibilities they have before and after each service. The team can discuss who will respond to pastoral needs from Seekers each week and whether team members will attend reception time following the service. Team members will also need to discuss how to be both friendly to Seekers and focused on the upcoming worship service before each service begins. Again, some of these aspects will begin to flow naturally after the team has worked together consistently. But initially, the team will be more comfortable and more effective if most of these roles and relationships are carefully outlined beforehand.

Finally, the team will want to share with one another their visions and hopes for this new ministry. Team members may even want to discuss what brought them to this new ministry.

Goals for the ministry can also be openly discussed at this stage to help team members and worship leaders evaluate the worship services and the ministry experience on an ongoing basis. Thinking through these types of plans and dreams together will further help to build a cohesive team.

Initial communications such as these are essential as this new ministry begins. But their value is not limited to early on in the process. These conversations should be continued throughout the worship planning process. In particular, new persons coming onto the team will need these conversations in order for new team members to discuss, reflect upon, and embrace the team's vision. If the vision is not shared by all the team members, the team will pull apart. Even the original team will find that re-igniting these types of conversations will help to keep the ministry fresh and vital, particularly at times when response levels are lower than expected or worship plans are not running smoothly.

Many models for the actual planning might be used, but my favorite model is noted below. I have used this model a number of times in traditional and contemporary settings to help a team start integrated planning. The model begins after the team has been chosen and begun meeting regularly to discuss the new ministry. The first planning meeting is usually set for an all-day or weekend retreat to allow ample time for the process to unfold naturally. In order to use this model, the team will need to come to the planning retreat with Bibles, hymnals, songbooks, song lists, drama books, video lists, and resources for prayers and other liturgical forms intended for use in the worship service.

A Model for Planning Seeker Worship

1. Prior to meeting, the preacher(s) and team leader(s) need to have prepared preliminary scripture and message outlines, along with the themes that arise from these scriptures and messages; musicians need to have

prepared repertoire lists as well as repertoire wish lists. If the team wishes to choose its own themes, the team will need to have done this prior to the planning retreat. The preacher would then choose scripture and message topics to correspond with the themes, still communicating all of this information prior to the retreat.

2. Team meets for a designated time period. A scribe or secretary is assigned to take notes on all ideas discussed. Tape recorders can also be helpful in this process, so that fleeting ideas can be re-captured as the planning process progresses.

3. Meeting opens with prayer and an overview of previous discussions about this new ministry with Seekers, the meaning of worship, and the vision/goals for this Seeker worship service.

4. Scriptures and themes are reviewed, along with images that come to mind from those scriptures and themes.

5. Message plans are outlined by the preacher(s), again allowing time for persons to share images and ideas that come to mind as the message plans are discussed.

6. Seasonal needs such as Christmas or Easter, school and church calendars, or specific community traditions are discussed and outlined. This can help the team keep in mind both the needs of Seekers and the traditions of the church into which the Seekers are to be integrated.

7. After these initial discussions, the team may choose to break into smaller groups to work on specific aspects of the worship services. If the team is small, these aspects can be planned by the entire team.

   a. Music leaders now begin choosing songs and/or hymns, keeping in mind thematic and scriptural emphases, musical abilities, sermon topics, congregational music preferences, and any desire for the introduction of new songs in a helpful way. Composers may begin making notes of specific services where new songs will be needed, or ideas they have for composing songs to correspond with certain themes. Musicians may begin thinking about special solos, songs by the band, or instrumental music that can become a part of the services. Some music teams choose a theme song for the worship service itself or for a specific season of the worship service. The theme song often opens or closes each worship service.

    b. Formal prayers and liturgical readings, if used, are written or chosen.

    c. Dramas, comedies, video plans, slide show ideas are introduced and discussed to correspond to certain services.

    d. Other artistic components are considered, such as dance during the message or a visual display prior to worship.

    e. Initial technical needs are discussed, while awaiting specific plans from the artists and worship leaders.

8. After the small groups have met, the entire team re-convenes to share the ideas. The scribe or secretary uses this time to collate ideas, often on an overhead transparency or newsprint. As the team sees the ideas integrated, the team will be better able to determine what flow will be most helpful and which ideas may need to be tabled for later use.

9. After the team begins to finalize worship plans for each of the services, the team leader (or another designated team member) reviews each service for integration and unity as well as diversity. Difficulties can then be shared with the entire team or with the appropriate small group for resolution.

10. Before the retreat comes to a close, detailed plans regarding specific services are discussed. At this point, the technical experts will have ideas and concerns to

be addressed. The team may even choose to use a flow chart to determine where extra workers are needed, who leaves the retreat with specific responsibilities, and how each service will be put into final form.

11. The retreat should end on an uplifting note, perhaps with a worship service. At the very least, the team will want to spend more time in prayer and song together before parting to begin the implementation process.

In planning worship for Seekers, the team will want to offer a high quality experience. Because of the team's diversity, this will be a very achievable goal. As the team plans, team members will find that ideas do not just come from the experts! Any team member may provide valuable input into any aspect of the service. A pastor may have an idea for a dramatic sketch to enhance a theme; a musician may have an insight into a message or theme as it relates to the congregation.

As the team plans, the team will also want to find ways to creatively integrate the church's traditions and heritage. Again, the importance of integrating Seekers with Followers will be a high motivation to find bridges between the "old" and the "new." The team will also want to offer opportunities for Seeker participation, not only in the worship setting but in other ministries of the church. Seekers may become important members of the Worship Planning Team, or Seekers may want to participate in the church's mission ministries. The worship team can provide a key contact point for Seekers by planning worship with these integration goals in mind.

The written and sung parts of worship that use affirming language and theology help Seekers to feel welcomed and appreciated. Likewise, the creativity and diversity reflected in the service will help to welcome the Seeker, particularly when the language and music are understandable.

Likewise, the worship leadership should be honest, open and genuine throughout each worship service. Words and actions need to reflect this authentic leadership style, so that Seekers will find the worship experience inviting and enjoyable. The very act of planning worship as a team will begin this process toward mutual ministry. The worship leadership team that functions as a small Body of Christ helps worship participants feel that everyone present is part of the larger Body of Christ. Seekers will almost always respond receptively to this type of warm atmosphere of friendship and partnership.

Just Do It: The Implementation Process

When the first worship service is opened to the public or the new ministry invites its first Seekers, the Implementation Stage has begun for the Planning and Nurturing Teams. (For the Marketing Team, however, the Implementation Stage actually begins several months earlier.) During the Implementation Stage, the Planning Team will begin coalescing as its members work together regularly to offer the worship service or ministry each week. At this stage, the ministry or worship service will begin to take on a life of its own as it becomes an ongoing ministry with Seekers. As the ministry matures, the Planning Team will certainly adapt to the changing information and knowledge gained from each new experience with Seekers. As Seekers begin to respond to the ministry, each Team (Planning, Marketing, Nurturing) will need to utilize evaluation tools to fine tune their skills and methods for reaching Seekers. Implementation is no easy task, but the energy and excitement of seeing the months of planning come to fruition will make it all worthwhile—particularly as the Teams see Seekers responding to the ministry and growing on the faith journey.

As the Worship Planning Team initiates its planning process for the first worship services, a Marketing Team should be implementing an advertising and evangelism plan. It is best if this outline was developed late in the investigation process. In so doing, implementation of the plan can occur quickly after the Investigating Team determines what type of service and ministry to offer Seekers. Marketing to Seekers is no easy task, but the resourceful Marketing Team will find ways of reaching Seekers appropriate to the Seeker needs in the community. Newspaper advertisements can be placed in the entertainment or living sections of the weekend paper. Ads may also be placed in entertainment guides in the community. Flyers at laundromats, grocery stores, bars, brew pubs, coffee shops, or other Seeker hangouts can also be very effective. Some Marketing Teams, particularly in urban areas, will want to actually distribute handbills on the street during lunch hours or rush hours as people are coming and going to and from work. Telephone campaigns may be effective with certain groups of Seekers, but formalized personal contact can be somewhat threatening or offensive to some Seekers. In almost any case, however, informal conversations in arenas where Seekers are likely to be comfortable are an effective means of inviting Seekers to a new worship service. This type of one-on-one contact, although time intensive and a heavy demand on personnel, may be your best means of gathering the initial group of Seekers for the new worship service. Radio or cable television ads need to be matched with the specific demographic group the worship service is designed to attract. Advertising a new alternative rock worship service during the *Lawrence Welk Show* on cable television is not likely to be very good use of the church's money or time! Initially, the Marketing Team will need to be very outward-looking in its efforts. However, over time, the Seekers who respond will become the best advertising outlet for the Marketing Team to utilize. At that point, invitational flyers can be made available to worship participants. Seekers who are connecting with the church can be encouraged, and even trained, about appropriate ways to share their experiences of this church with friends in the community. Some Seekers may become very effective members of the Marketing Team, helping to reach other Seekers who are likely to respond to the new ministry. As the worship service is implemented and develops a life of its own, the Marketing Team's work will grow and respond to the worship service and to the worshippers who attend the service. As with the planning process, marketing or advertising or evangelism efforts must be evaluated and adjusted regularly.

The Joy of Going Into All the World

The ministry may grow beyond anyone's expectations, and with that growth new ideas and changes in plans will need to be implemented. Original plans may even need to be discarded. A Worship Planning Team or Marketing Team that insists on sticking to a regimented proposal, even when the plan is floundering, is not likely to be effective in reaching Seekers on any type of ongoing basis. Enjoy the fluidity of this challenging and changing ministry. Revel in the opportunity to experiment and try new things. Share the joys and sorrows with one another, realizing that strongly unified and supportive teams offer a beautiful model of a well-functioning Body of Christ. And, praise God for the successes that bring fulfillment and the failures that bring new knowledge to this ministry. Each worship service, each Seeker, each new stage on the journey will bring growth and challenge, improvement and change.

Ministry with Seekers is a new opportunity for the 21st century, because Seekers are a different breed of people than the church has been addressing in recent years. As the world around us changes abruptly and unexpectedly over the next few years, the needs and interests of Seekers are likely to change as well. Thus, effective worship experiences for Seekers and ministry with Seekers will be those that are flexible and responsive to the changing world. As we search for Seekers, reach out to Seekers, and begin to understand the Seekers in our midst, we will learn new ways of being in ministry. We will discover information and ideas that no author has yet discovered. Integrating the new ideas, relevant information, and creative ways to search for and reach Seekers will help our ministries with Seekers to grow and develop into wonderful places of mutual growth on the Christian journey.

Yes, Seeker worship and ministry with Seekers is filled with ups and downs. Any church entering into the Search for Seekers simply as a means of gaining new converts and reversing a downward trend in membership or participation levels will surely be disappointed. But for Followers who develop a passion for reaching Seekers—no matter what the cost—ministry and worship with Seekers will bring fulfillment and growth that are immeasurable. The Search for Seekers is itself a growth opportunity, a chance for Followers to learn more about who we are, who God is calling us to be, and how we are able to live out that calling. Much like the father of the Prodigal Son, Followers who search for Seekers will find that the search itself increases our ability to love others as Christ has loved us. Amy Grant and her songwriting team remind us of this poignant reality in the song, "The Prodigal":

> And when I finally see you come
> I'll run when I see you. . . . I'll meet you.[2]

And so, I leave you with the hope that you will find, as I have found with Michael, that your ability to love matures and grows throughout the search. My prayer is that the Search for Seekers *will* result in reaching Seekers, so that Seekers and Followers alike may experience this maturity in love of God and neighbor. Together, we are all better able to walk this Christian journey toward health and wholeness in unity with God and one another. Whatever form your ministry with Seekers takes over the next few years, you will find that the ministry will be filled with new opportunities, unexpected challenges, and rewarding experiences. Go, therefore, into all of the communities of the world. Search for Seekers, inviting them onto the journey of following Christ. Offer the saving grace of Christ Jesus, and teach Seekers and Followers the way of following Christ. Rest (and work) assured that Christ is with all of us—Seeker and Follower alike—always, even until the end of the world!

Notes

1. Special thanks to David Huether and Paige Meili, entrepreneurial consultants, who outlined this process for me.

2. Listen to "The Prodigal" ("I'll Be Waiting") from *Amy Grant: Unguarded*. Copyright 1985 Bug and Bear Music, Fred and Ethel Music Company, Nanacub Music.

Just the Basics, Please

Seekers Need Community

- A Community of Faith, in which to continue their spiritual journeys
- A Community of Growth, where Seekers and Followers mature to a greater love of God and neighbor
- A Community of Support, to combat the loneliness pervasive in our society and to pursue the spiritual journey with companions and mentors
- A Community of Acceptance, where doubts and questions can be explored openly and where differences in dress and attitude can be tolerated
- A Community of Understanding, where Seekers are allowed to "learn as we go" and not expected to know everything in order to participate in the community
- A Community of Christians, persons who live and express meaningful reasons for turning to Christ as our Companion-Guide for the journey of faith

Seekers Look For:

- Community
- Spiritual Nourishment
- Theological Challenge
- Safe Places to Explore Questions & Doubts
- A Relevant Message of Good News
- A Reason for Turning to Christ

Reaching Seekers of Different Generations

When ministering with Seekers, our ministries will often need to be designed with the needs of a specific generation of Seekers in mind. On the following chart, church leaders can begin to explore and understand specific needs of Seekers in each generation.

Mature Generations (Builders & Balancers; born 1901–1942)	Boomer Generation (born 1943–1960)	Busters & Birthers (born 1961 -Present)

• Connection with a Community of Faith
• Acceptance & Forgiveness
• A Place to Ask Difficult Questions:
  • Who am I?
  • Why am I here?
  • What will I leave behind?
  • What does death mean?
  • What is God?
  • What does God have to do with me?
	• A Community of Stability and Integrity
	• Peace of Mind
	• A Place of Nurture
	• A Place to Ask Challenging Questions
	  • Am I making a difference?
	  • Where is God?
	  • How can I find sanity in such a busy life?
	  • Why do I need God or others?
	  • Who will my children become?
	  • How do I care for my aging parents?
	  • Will I die alone?
		• A Relevant Community of Faith & Authenticity
		• Acceptance & Companionship
		• A Place to Build Relationships
		• A Place to Express Talent & Creativity
		• A Place to be Useful
		• A Place to Explore Questions & Doubts
		  • Who am I?
		  • Who is God?
		  • Does God make any difference?
		  • Where do I fit in & what is my purpose?
		  • How do I develop meaningful relationships?
		  • Whom can I trust?
		  • Do people care?
		  • How do I help my children to care for others?

Mature Generations	Boomer Generation	Busters & Birthers
• Worship that connects to their experience	• Worship that connects to their experience	• Worship that connects to their experience
• Traditional Hymns	• Pop Music and Light Rock of High Quality	• Diverse, complex music, often secular
• Quality Music	• Slower Pace, with High Stimulus, often with High Energy Leadership	• High energy leadership in a fast-pace setting
• Time for Silence	• Practical, Non-judgmental Messages	• Relevant Messages
• Honest, Non-Judgmental Messages		

Seeker Friendly Churches

- Train Ushers & Greeters in the art of welcoming Seekers & Followers
- Train Worship Leaders in the art of leading welcoming worship
- Constantly evaluate the use of language and communication tools, striving to avoid language that excludes Outsiders and striving to use language that welcomes all
- Utilize written communication that is "user-friendly" with lots of white space, readable print fonts, hints on participation (such as printed words to memorized prayers, Bible page numbers or instructions when to stand), and notepads or guidelines on listening to and participating in the message
- Share basic information about communicating, such as the church address and phone number and the pastor's name in all written communications and advertisements
- Express a warm sense of hospitality with tasty food, comfortable reception areas, and friendly Followers who interact with Seekers and Followers alike

SEEKER FRIENDLY WORSHIP INCLUDES ALL THE BASICS FOR WELCOMING SEEKERS

- Understandable worship language and message themes Integration of secular resources and language into the sacred experience
- Written and verbal instructions that explain everything expected of the worshiper (when to sit, when to stand, when to sing, when to speak)
- Multiple means of communicating (verbal and visual—written in handouts or songbooks, written on overhead or video projections, and displayed in artwork and physical gestures)
- Friendly greeters and ushers who can and do offer guidance and instruction about all aspects of the worship service and church offerings
- Worship and music leadership that is warm and welcoming
- Sacraments that are offered to, but not required of, all participants
- Comfortable seating areas, with easy access for those who wish to leave during the worship service
- Clear directional signs to restrooms, nursery areas, parking, worship space, and reception area

Making The Move Toward Becoming a Seeker Friendly Church

Few, if any, churches in this country are achieving a total Seeker-Friendly atmosphere. Rather, churches that are reaching Seekers are striving to be as welcoming as possible. As you move toward becoming more Seeker-Friendly, consider integrating the following ideas gradually or quickly into the life of as a place where Seekers are welcomed and integrated into an accepting Community of Faith.

- Train church leadership (ushers, greeters, officers, worship leaders) in the basics & the art of welcoming and communicating with Seekers
- Develop "Seeker-Sensitive Eyes" to help discover and correct the unwelcoming aspects of your church and worship settings
- Integrate "cues" into your worship services: written and/or verbal instructions that help people to worship even when they are unfamiliar with your church traditions
- Educate Followers about the needs of Seekers in your community

Urban Settings

- May need to concentrate on socio-economic needs as well as spiritual needs
- May reach a greater number of young and unmarried Seekers
- May already have more ability to communicate with lively music and relevant messages
- May need to be particularly aware of avoiding dependence on written communication (to address issues of illiteracy and multilingualism)

Suburban Settings

- May need to concentrate on developing less stressful alternatives to hectic lifestyles, in addition to addressing spiritual needs
- May reach a greater number of Seeker families, often by reaching the teenagers first
- May need to overcome strong institutional biases toward "correct" church music or "appropriate" church dress codes
- May find educational and community service offerings an excellent way of reaching Seekers

Rural Settings

- May need to be very intentional about advertising to Seekers, to avoid stereotypes that the church is only for those who were born into that setting
- May reach a greater number of older Seekers
- May need to help Followers overcome insistence on certain church traditions, such as favorite seating areas or insistence on "old favorite" memorized hymns or prayers

Turning to Christ: A Dramatic Dialogue Based on the Healing in Mark 5:25–34

Preacher as Neighbor to the Healed Woman

I don't really know how many doctors she had been to see. But, for as long as I could remember, she'd been sick. The constant hemorrhage caused pain and inconvenience, but worse than any of that her illness left her an outcast. To bleed like that all the time every month, year after year—every one knew that a woman was unclean when that happened. Who knows what some people thought? Even her family refused to see her! They must have been afraid of what the neighbors would say. But, now she's a different person. I didn't realize how bright and funny she could be. I guess I wasn't really any better than anyone else—even though I rented a room to her for all those years, I did overcharge her because of the embarrassment she caused me. Now that I'm an old woman, she takes care of me—and she doesn't blame me for my aches and pains. She certainly doesn't charge me for any of the work she does for me. I really don't understand who she is anymore, she's so warm and kind, not bitter and angry the way she used to be, and I sure love her. But, I'm not supposed to be telling her story.

Here she comes now . . . I think she'd rather speak for herself. She's like that you know, likes to tell what she's seen and felt. Rebecca, some people came by again today . . . they heard you knew that Jesus fellow and want to hear all about it.

Preacher as the Woman

I can't say that I really knew him. It was more like he knew me. I still remember the day I met him—It was a beastly hot day. Usually, the summer's aren't too bad around here—you can count on a nice breeze off the shore. But the day he was in town, there was no breeze. Just hot sticky air—kind of like today. But, the heat didn't seem to be any worse for me than the cold. Everything made me miserable. Or I let everything make me miserable. Oh, I had some terrible stomach pains, but I knew that this Jesus guy was out in the center of town speaking. I thought maybe he could help me. Heaven knows the doctors hadn't found any cures for me. And the rabbis wouldn't even set foot in my apartment because of my bleeding. Oh, I'd thought about going to a witch doctor or one of the marketplace physicians, but most of the ones I heard about were just traveling pranksters—out for a denarrius. Money wasn't too easy to come by for me. I couldn't find work in anyone's home since I was always unclean. The only work I could do was out of my own home, and even then my customers couldn't know who was doing the work. When I mended clothes or made trinkets for people, I always had to pay some errand boy an exorbitant wage to run back and forth to customers. If they'd had any idea who was doing their mending or what was wrong with me, they'd have taken their business elsewhere. And, the errand boys didn't like to touch my work, but for enough money they would cover for me and run my merchandise back and forth and even find customers for me. But, money was usually tight.

But, I'd heard that Jesus didn't take money from people; sometimes he even gave money to people! Now don't get me wrong, I wasn't going to beg for money. I just wanted to see him, to hear him, just to touch him would be enough to relieve some of the pain—I was sure. But when I left that morning, I never realized I'd come home a new woman. There I go, getting ahead of myself again.

Anyway, off I went to the marketplace to look for a new errand boy, but I didn't have much luck with that search. Then I went to find Jesus. It wasn't too hard—even the market looked empty compared to the crowd that Jesus had attracted. Oh, it was so hard to fight that crowd though. I couldn't even get close enough to see him. Fortunately, the big crowd kept me safe from being noticed by someone who knew me and might send me home as unclean. So, I kept edging my way in closer to Jesus. Sometimes the pain would stab through me like a knife, especially if I ran into an elbow or someone's walking stick.

But, as I listened to Jesus and moved closer little by little, I began to believe that this effort might actually prove worthwhile. For some reason, I began to see that I could be healed. I could be a whole person again—if only I could move close enough to touch him. Well, no I'd never be able to touch him—then he might notice and I'd be sent home when the crowd saw who I was. I'd heard that Jesus even camped with the lepers, so I knew that he wouldn't mind being touched by me—but he might notice and single me out. And the crowd would mind that I was there! So, as I worked my way toward Jesus, I thought that I would just try to touch his sleeve. Even that small contact could heal me. I just knew it!

Just as I moved up to Jesus, someone jabbed me with their elbow. Oh, I guess they didn't mean it—probably didn't even know what they'd done in such close quarters. But, you know how someone can hit you in just the right place and the breath just seems to leave you. That happened to me; the pain shot through my stomach and up through my throat and I fell to the ground. But once I was that close to Jesus, I wasn't about to lose my chance. So, I started to crawl toward him. It was almost easier to crawl than to walk because I could squeeze between people's legs more easily than between their bodies. But I feared I'd be stepped on at any moment. Yet, I knew if I could even touch the hem of his garment that I could be whole again. I'd have a new life—an opportunity to start over without the bleeding, with good health and another chance to meet people, to work, to go to worship, everything. Well, Jesus stopped to talk to someone and that gave me the time I needed to reach out and touch his garment. As soon as I did, I felt so warm. The pain in my stomach was gone, the blood that had been flowing down my legs ever since I fell to the ground stopped right then. Can you believe it? I just jumped up right in the middle of the crowd and started to cry for joy.

But before I could move back away from Jesus and avoid being noticed, he turned around like a flash and said "Who touched my garments?" Just what I had feared, if he realized it was me the whole crowd would see me and someone would recognize me as the woman with the ceaseless hemmorhage! Those people who were always with Jesus, his assistants, I guess, tried to tell him that anyone could have touched him in this close crowd. But, I knew that Jesus knew it was me. So, I walked up to Jesus. I was so scared then. For the first time, I feared that he might be angry that I had touched him, so I fell on my knees before him and told him everything as quickly as I could—how I'd been sick for so very long, how I knew that just touching his robe could heal me, how I didn't want to bother him or be noticed by the crowd.

> There was nowhere else to turn,
> And nowhere else to go;
> My body knew all the pain
> A body can know,
> When I quietly turned to you,
> I quietly turned to you,
> Help of the helpless,
> I turned to you.

When no one else would help,
And no one else could hear
My cries full of anguish,
My cries full of fear,
Then I quietly turned to you,
I quietly turned to you,
Hope of the hopeless,
I turned to you.

I saw you standing there,
I saw the beauty from
you beaming,
I saw the peace, the joy, the perfect love that
could be.
I saw you standing there,
I thought that I was surely dreaming:
For suddenly warmth and love and joy were shin-
ing through me
As you quietly turned to me,
You quietly turned to me,
Friend of the friendless,
You turned to me.[1]

And, he did the most amazing thing of all.He took me by the hand—a Jewish man touching an unclean, unmarried woman by the hand, can you believe it?! Anyway, he took me by the hand and lifted me to my feet. Then, he looked at me with the biggest, kindest eyes I've ever seen. But, those eyes pierced right through me—I felt like he knew every doubt and fear and anger that I'd ever felt and that he understood every last one of them. But then, he didn't say anything about all of those hurts, he said, "Daughter, your faith has made you well." My faith, my hope, my dreams?! I thought they were all fairy tales to be ignored, but he said that my faith had made me well. "Go in peace, and be healed of your disease," he said to me. He wasn't just talking about my hemorrhaging for all those years, he meant the peaceless existence that I'd lived all of those years. Hiding in dark corners when people came to my land-lady's house, sneaking through back alleys to run my errands, paying errand boys to keep my secret, feeling alone and un-wanted by everyone I'd ever known. He said that my faith could remedy all of that. And, you know, he was right. Faith can remedy all of that. Faith that God can work in me and through me, the hope and the belief that Jesus, the Christ, can save me and heal me and forgive me and continues to do so every day. Sometimes that faith seems further away than other days, sometimes Jesus' touch seems further away than other days, but I try to remember that I will feel that closeness again. Sometimes, I have to spend a lot of time reaching out to other people to rediscover that faith. When I can see God working in other people—no matter how outcast and downtrodden, or popular and wealthy those people may be—when I see God with them or help them to see God, it reminds me that God is with me as well. It's not always easy; but it's better than it used to be. I know that my faith is real and that Jesus really did touch me, really did speak to me—when I turned to him, he was there.

> Now I know such perfect peace,
> I feel such sweet release,
> Your love let me live again,
> Your love set me free.
> Help of the helpless,
> Friend of the friendless,
> I quietly turned to you,
> And you turned to me,
> And you turned to me.[2]

Notes

1. "I Quietly Turned to You," from the musical, "Celebrate Life," by Ragan Courtney and Buryl Red. Copyright 1972, Hope Publishing Company.
2. Ibid.